FREE-lancing

Shaping your mind, Planning your business

Winnie Carmo

Please, get your **FREE GIFT**, a workbook that will help you make the most of this book.

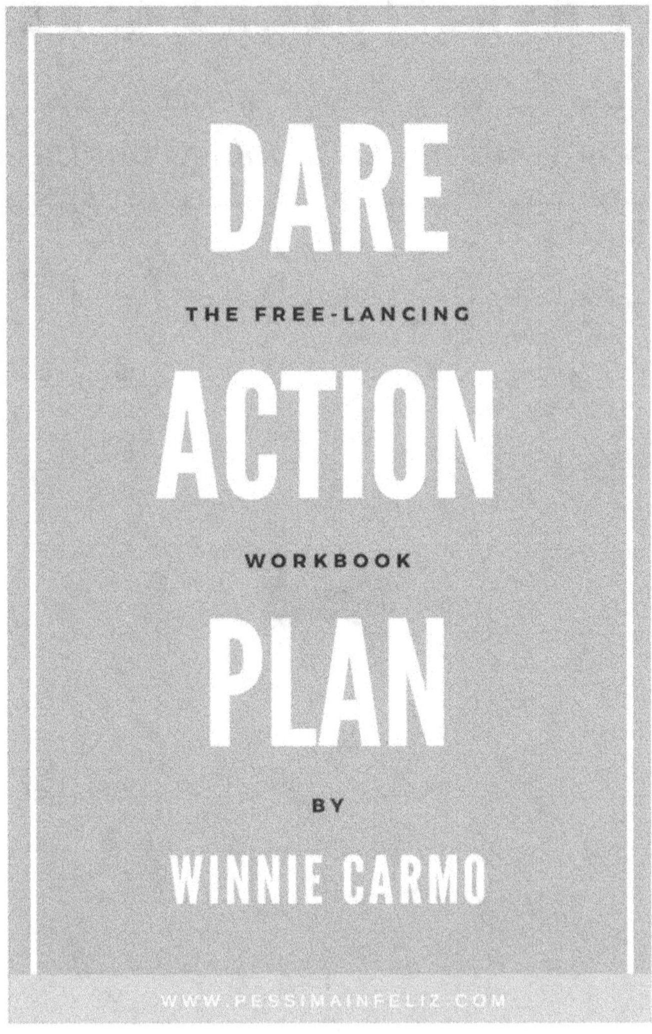

Available at: https://aw16d4ac.aweberpages.com/p/8f8fa9e7-d36c-4223-8e6d-08542f27fa87

www.pessimainfeliz.com
Cover Design by: www.BookJoJo.com
Interior Design by: www.BookJoJo.com
ISBN: 978-989-54785-0-7

Dedication

This book is dedicated to my life partner, **Evandro Ferreira**, who made me see myself as a writer and encouraged me to make a career out of my craft.

To my father**, Carmo Neto**, who did a great job passing me the genes to be a writer and awaken the avid reader in me since childhood.

To my mother, **Ana Paula Carmo**, who always believed in my potential and supported my choices.

To my sister, **Cássia Carmo**, who saw the author in me before myself, and who's a brilliant writer herself.

To my little sister, **Hélia Carmo**, who gave me more admiration than I deserve and made me impersonate the saying "leading by example".

CONTENTS

Introduction

Do you feel chained to that job that you hate, worried that there's no solution for you? Are you jobless and think you will be for the foreseeable future since companies have been dismissing people to cut down costs? Does your professional life seem out of your control and that dream of professional realization is not even on the horizon anymore, right?

You can take matters into your own hands, and finally be free as a professional who can make a great living. You can earn the income you feel you deserve and do it from anywhere you choose to be. You can do it on your own terms. That's what freelancing is about — to realize one's professional dream and grow in unimaginable ways.

I'm not talking about a magic formula that will allow you to ditch your unemployed status overnight or kiss your boss goodbye tomorrow, but I'm talking about you exerting your right to professional freedom and choosing to build your own future.

Because of my journey into the freedom of freelancing, I decided I wanted to show people everywhere, including my home country of Angola, that they could build their own professional lives and *always* find an alternative to feeling stuck at work.

But then, you may ask: "Is it possible to make a living as a freelancer?" "Is that a respectable profession?" "How do you even get started?" "I support my whole family, I couldn't even begin to think about not having a traditional job!"

Because of the internet, you can become a freelancer no matter where you live. You can do work for people all over the world, from all over the world. So, whether you're Angolan, American, or British, this book is for you. In this book, I show you not only how to set your mindset for success as a freelancer, but also which steps to take to prepare yourself before starting your freelance career. I also mention the main areas to invest heavily in to have a regular income, as well as how to deal with the ups and downs of freelance life.

I believe in practice over theory and the steps I share are actionable and straight forward. Thus, I'm offering you the Dare Action Plan, a free workbook I have specifically designed to give you a little push in implementing what you learn. I'd also recommend you use the resources I made available on my blog (https://pessimainfeliz.com/resources/).

As an ambitious-and-eager-to-learn-and-share type of person, I have developed my working methods and strategies, based on avid reading and tireless implementation of best practices. I have managed to solidify my own structure as a freelancer and have built a customer list that includes well-known and highly respected local and international institutions.

I have no doubt freelancing is a secure way to be successful because it's a one-person job. You can finish reading this book today and start taking action the minute you finish it. Additionally, I also provide a very clear picture of what you should do, when it'd be best to go ahead, and how to make the most of your experience.

Only after I became a freelancer was I able to be completely independent and take a much-dreamed road trip around Angola, work for national and international political personalities, and even save enough money to stop working for a few years, if I wanted to.

By reading this book, you will be able to avoid mistakes I made myself. You will be able to start your freelancing journey quickly and gain financial independence, all while enjoying what you do. If you follow the simple steps illustrated in this guide, you will nourish the best relationships, find customers, and achieve professional goals that you set for yourself.

Since you picked up this book, you're looking for a solution, for your professional self 2.0. Don't be the person who stays on the edge, watching everyone else take action while you stay behind. Instead, be the one who leads the way, creates possibilities, and inspires others. You can think of freelancing as your ticket to world citizenship.

Have a sneak peek at what the book covers and then jump straight into what will be your next step.

Part 1: Before you become a freelancer

This part of the book is about building the right mindset and thinking about the essential areas of success to start your freelancing activity. You will be prompted to deeply analyze the real purpose for wanting to go freelance, whether in a part-time or full-time capacity. It will also help you see your best qualities and truly make a commitment to your goal.

Obviously, your finances should be one of the first things you check before consolidating your decision, even though money should not be the main reason for you to take the jump. Doing research is just as important and designing a business plan will make you see things realistically.

In this part, I also talk about how to go about creating a business structure and drafting a good business plan, in order to have everything on paper and look at it from an objective and accurate point of view. You will learn different ways to test your freelancer competences before quitting your job and how to handle resigning your office job in a manner that will keep the doors open, should you want to return.

Part 2: How to manage freelancing

In the second part of the book, I teach you how to start your freelance activity by setting your goals, organizing them, and getting your working space sorted. This section goes into how to deal with customers by guiding you through best practices to attract, manage, and retain your clients.

I will then talk to you about time management, to save you from overloading yourself and making the newbie mistake of working through the night. If you adopt a clever methodology of work, you will achieve efficiency and buy yourself precious time.

The following chapters focus on the financial part of the business, as a way of grounding the health and sustainability of it. You'll also learn tips to staying financially safe and secure, even if you get just a few customers.

In the end, I address a potential freelancer fear: not making it, struggling as a freelancer. The tips I give here are based on my own experience, offering you unique and truthful examples of how to overcome tough situations in this occupation.

Part 3: The reality of being a freelancer

Here I talk in-depth about the reality of being a freelancer, with the pros and cons of this professional lifestyle, including what nobody else will tell you.

How to make the most of this book

As you read each chapter, use the Dare Action Plan Workbook to do the corresponding exercises and check the resources page (https://pessimainfeliz.com/resources/) to fully absorb the contents of the book and practice as you learn.

There are also points to keep in mind at the end of each chapter. I'd advise you to write them down or print them out and stick them on the wall or on your computer screen as a "take-away" message for you to implement in your life.

As you can tell, all you have to do is sit tight and read the first chapter.

PART I

Before the Parachute Launch

"If you become a successful entrepreneur you will come to know a freedom very few people will ever know. The freedom from the fear of freedom itself."

— Robert Kiyozaki

Freelancing is the state of being self-employed and autonomous in your professional life. Because of this, many are motivated to go freelance to achieve professional freedom as opposed to money or career goals, even though those are generally strong elements in the equation as well.

In today's world, freelancing has no limits. Think of the one thing you like doing the most right now. Indulge in it and enjoy how it makes you feel. The very same thing you thought of can be your freelancing practice, whatever it is. If you don't believe me, google it this instant, and test my theory. Play around with the words a little and chances are you will find out that your beloved hobby can be turned into a profession and there are already different formats and subcategories for it. Plus, there are people living on it and making serious money. Then, why aren't you one of them? What are you waiting for?

As a freelancer, you're in control of your workload, having the freedom to reject or accept as many projects as you like; you decide when, where, and for whom to work. Additionally, you can avoid long commutes or even relocate to the place you would most like to live and offer your services from there.

When managed well, freelancing can be great for your mental and physical health and give you a sense of purpose and fulfillment in life. It can help you align your values and beliefs with your day-to-day activities.

All you need right now is to determine your deepest motivation for wanting to go freelance, acknowledge your best qualities and weak points, ditch what's holding you back, make a commitment to yourself, and get down to the numbers in a solid business plan. Brace yourself, I will guide you through it all.

From the Inside Out

CHAPTER 1

Identify your why

There is a Paulo Flores'[1] song, *Inocenti* (Innocent or Naïve, in this case), sings about a boy who claims to know nothing, but to be a beggar.

It is a particularly touching song for me because it speaks of child who's lost and doesn't feel they have a place in the world . . . they are not even aware they can choose their own path.

Just like this song suggests, many young orphans felt they could not choose their own path. I had the opportunity to work for a while with the manager of a boys' orphanage. He told me that the percentage of kids who end up going through the entire school program through the orphanage is less than 30 percent. That's because most of them are so used to earning quick money on the streets that staying in a shelter, following rules, and having a vision is something completely new for them.

Most of us, who live in the city of Luanda, Angola, give money on a daily basis to one of those kids, to either wash our cars or carry our heavy shopping bags. When they ask for a more regular commitment and you give them a job, they are very

---

[1] One of Angolans most respected songwriters and singers

enthusiastic in the beginning, but most of them go back to street jobs or just disappear. Survival mode is all they know; it's home for them.

Thinking long term is no easy task, reflecting on who you are and what your goals are requires planning, careful implementation, willpower, and sacrifices. But if you're willing to cover long distances in life, you will need the power generator to keep your lights on and your head up.

Don't be like *Inocenti* and resign yourself to being a beggar. Instead, be a go-getter. Start by finding your main drive.

Unveiling your why

If you want to turn your dream into a full-time job, know that your dream will only become a reality if you understand why it is your dream. What makes you want to live that dream? What is the major force that drives you to do it?

To be honest, before I became a freelancer, I had not clearly identified my goal. Years later, I have come to understand myself better and actually find my why.

All of us believe in something. It doesn't matter if you're religious or not, if you believe in God, Allah, Buddha, the Universe; if your family is your reason to be; or if you just believe in the goodness of people or in your mother's delicious meals. Everyone has something that drives them and that is the why. What change do you want to make in the world? What direction do you want your life to take?

What really worked for me was an exercise from the book *Millionaire Success Habits*, by Dean Graziosi, called "The 7 Levels Deep." It requires you to ask *why* seven times, using the previous answer as the baseline for the next question. Don't ask me why seven times; it just works!

I started with the question on their website "What is important to you about becoming successful?" As I progressed, the answers to the *why* were more emotional and instinctive and required less thinking. In the end, I realized that the roots of my main motivation were very patriotic; it had to do with living up to the expectations of those who fought for Angola to be a free country. I do not want that struggle to be in vain. We fought for so many years for this country to be a free nation that now I feel I have the duty to defend the Angolan freedom and show the Angolan citizens how we can build up this country together.

It was a realization, an important discovery; I didn't know that was my core why. Now I have a different drive and commitment. I want to create a legacy, not for myself but for future generations.

Another way you can work on finding your why is by following the tips and exercises Simon Sinek gives in *Finding Your Why*. They all begin with remembering the most remarkable stories of your past, good and bad. For instance, he tells the story of a woman who had a traumatic childhood with abusive parents.

When she told her stories, of moments she found happiness and sorrow, she realized all she was trying to do all the time was to protect her little sister, shield her from that horror. No wonder she became a lawyer and worked with clients in similar situations.

When I was six years old my mom asked me what I wanted to be when I grew up:

— "Winnie, what do you want to be when you grow up?"

— "I want to be a lawyer," I answered, chin up, eyes defiant.

— "Why do you want to be a lawyer?"

— "To defend the poor!"

— "Oh honey, that's not how the world works."

Funny thing, I still want to work to help others. The difference is now, 25 years later, I know I can!

In this "remembering past stories" exercise, try putting together as many stories as possible (15-20); just jot down the memories on a piece of paper as they come to you. No filter!

Regardless of the process you choose to follow to identify your why, you should take a few things into consideration:

1. Be open to the process and let yourself be vulnerable. That is, you have to be willing to open up to things that may hurt you. But, most of all, be open to the unknown,

your inner self, your thoughts, your emotions. It's very important that you face yourself as a whole.

2. Find a physical space you like, that allows you to be at peace. It should be quiet to allow you to self-reflect, without judgment, and without self-criticism. Focus on looking deep.

3. Let it flow naturally; don't wear the "perfection cap." Write freely until you no longer feel you have anything to add.

4. Read it straight away, but don't delete anything, let it be.

5. Put it away and give it at least 3–5 days before you read it again so you can gain more perspective.

6. If you decide to do the exercise with somebody else, make sure it's someone who knows you very well but who is not afraid to tell you the absolute truth about yourself.

Reflect on these experiences to help you identify your why

Going after what you want is scary, daunting, and sometimes might feel like it's just impossible. However, worse than that is feeling like a certain situation has taken over your life and you've lost control of it.

I believe in possibilities, mind over matter, and facing your challenges. Therefore, I strongly recommend you eliminate the following reason as *your* "why":

1. "I need more money. I can barely make rent!"

Of course, we all need money to live. But freelancing is not a quick way to make money or a magic formula; it's a long-term commitment, a life-long career. So, if you think of freelancing as a short-term gig, chances are, you've set yourself up for failure. But if you're planning to take it seriously, you will need something more important than money to drive you. Focusing on financial gain as your only motivator will not bring you long-term happiness and fulfillment.

You have much better chances of making it work if you view it as a purpose, a life mission. Work on yourself to become better at what you do, then you *and* your business will grow.

When you learn how to make money, even if you lose it, you'll always have the knowledge to regain it. Obviously, there are many other factors that come into play, but if you know your values, strengths, and weaknesses, chances are you'll know how to create money and how to use your tools in your favor.

2. "I hate my boss/company/job."

I hate to break it to you (no, I don't, somebody has to!), but not wanting to work for your boss, your company, or anyone else in general is *not* a reason strong enough for you to leave your job to be a freelancer. You need much more than that. You really need to know what you want and why.

A friend of mine got in touch with me the other day, asking for tips on becoming a freelancer and the whole process I went through. After answering her, I asked why she wanted to become a freelancer. And, as I expected, she was unhappy at her job.

I said "Think again! Rushing into an unknown because you're desperately running away from something may be the equivalent of your own hell."

Freelancing isn't a way to get out of a trap, although it might be arguable. If you've lost your job and are just trying to keep your head above water, please, take a breath and trust everything will be OK. Keep breathing and let your beautiful brain do the work. Rushing into something you don't know you will enjoy or profit from will just make you want to have your head underwater.

Make the most of the fact that you have people who love you in your life and ask if you can rely on them while you're finding your way back into self-sustainability. Just don't take too long. They have a life too and you're supposed to rely on them, not lay down and roll on them.

Keep in mind . . .

- You have a purpose in life, and you can find it; you just need to unveil your why
- Think of money as your servant, _never_ as your mentor!

- Your boss and/or company might be the very definition of hell, but do not let them be the reason for your self-made nightmare

- Fight or flight is a survival mode attitude. Don't be reactive, be proactive and act with intention.

CHAPTER 2

Identify your strengths and weaknesses

Now that you know how to find your why, zoom into your strengths and weaknesses. Think about your professional and personal life so far, and as you do, jot things down under the categories of strengths and weaknesses. Consider both hard skills (such as things you learn in school) and soft skills (character traits like being personable or organized). Do this with the help of some of the people you're closest to, so you get the full picture. You can also ask for the thoughts of current or past coworkers. It may be more challenging than you think, but it will be worth it.

Reflect on:

- your good and bad moments

- your challenges and what came easy

- what you need help with and what others come to you for help

- what is satisfying and what is a drag

- how do you deal with your colleagues, friends, and family?

Dean Graziosi, in *Millionaire Success Habits*, suggests that instead of trying to improve your performance on the things you do poorly, you should focus on what you already do well. That is, if you're a great writer and a crappy file organizer, just focus on your writing and get someone you know will do a five-star organization job on your files. He advocates that this increases your confidence and, consequently, makes you see yourself as capable rather than feeling guilty for the things you can't or don't feel motivated to do.

This premise aligns with what was found thanks to a computer setting mistake at a US university. In *The 7 Habits of Highly Effective People* by Stephen Covey, he tells about a group of students who took an IQ test in their first semester. Some scored low and some scored high. When, five months later, they discovered an error in the scoring, they realized that those who got good results should have scored low and vice-versa.

The students took the exam again, without being told why. Surprisingly, those who mistakenly received the high scores previously performed well and those who mistakenly received low scores previously did poorly. The professors concluded that the group who performed poorly had started seeing themselves as less intelligent people. With the other group, the opposite happened. They viewed themselves as smart and acted accordingly, obtaining much better results. So choose your mirror wisely, for it can make you or destroy you.

Keep in mind . . .

- Focus on developing your strengths.

- Be mindful of the lens through which you see the world.

CHAPTER 3

Get rid of excuses and take action

Having identified your strengths and weakness, you're now equipped with the knowledge of who you are and what you're capable of. So, what is keeping you from taking the next steps?

A while ago, a good friend of mine came to me and started talking about how she came to be in what my sister would call a "situationship," that is, a relationship that is never going to happen. The conversation went something like this:

— "You know that guy I like? We spent a month in Costa Rica, but nothing happened," she said, almost holding her breath.

— "What?! How come? I mean, you're the full package."

— "I think it was because we were with another friend, and this girl liked him too and was jealous of me. She wouldn't leave us alone for two minutes."

— "Girlfriend, most Angolans have babies by the time the clock hits minute one."

— "I know" — she said giggling — "But I think he's insecure, and his last relationship ended really badly. Plus, I never really told him how I feel about him."

— "And what's stopping you?" I asked

— "Some friends say I look too desperate and that turns him off. I want to tell him, but he has been really busy, I'm about to be away for a couple of weeks, then it's the holiday season."

— "Kima, all you're telling me is that life will keep happening while you wait for the perfect moment to live." I heard my words making their way into her brain, causing an almost visible pain.

Many of us put off what we want with any excuse we can find, whether plausible or not. Truth is, any excuse is a setback in what we truly want to accomplish.

In many realities, it's very common for young adults to support their parents and even siblings, which may make them feel they are deprived of their own dreams and wants.

While I totally understand that the role of the main provider is highly demanding, I still agree with Ricardo Kaniama (the African Robert Kiyozaki), in *A Cabra Da Minha Mãe* (My mom's goat), when he says that this self-entitled dependence only contributes to the laziness and lack of responsibility of those who deliberately choose to wait for the fruits of your work to survive. I invite you to see your desire as an opportunity for all of your dependants to get on board with you and create a scenario of mutual help.

If you are all in the same boat, you will all be responsible for its stability in the water. To do that, you will need to take the wheel and explain the situation to gain their cooperation. I know families can be very challenging and resist the idea of a provider wanting to follow their dream and putting the survival of the whole family at risk, but your success is *your* responsibility.

Think of it as a movie. Today, you're in an unhappy situation, you work for a company that doesn't align with your values and follow orders you don't believe will make the world a better place. Fast-forward 10 years from now. Can you see yourself in the same situation? Doing the same job, working with the same people and going to the same office? Is that what you want for yourself?

Keep in mind . . .

- Life doesn't take breaks, waiting for you to figure things out.

- It takes perseverance to live a life of abundance and get everyone on board.

- If you don't like the movie you're watching, don't waste your time. You have the power to change it.

CHAPTER 4

Write a personal mission statement

After you ditched the excuses and decided to make your life a better place to be, you're ready to make a commitment to yourself and write a mission statement or make a vision board that will keep you energized.

A personal mission statement is a written commitment you make with yourself, stating what you want to do, why you want to do it, and how you will make it happen.

A practice I read in *Think and Grow Rich*, by Napoleon Hill, triggers you to focus on your big goal and reminds you of what you will need to do to achieve it. By incorporating each of the main parts below you can create a solid mission statement:

1. What you want to accomplish
2. By when (deadline)
3. What you're willing to do or give up in exchange
4. A visualization of what it means to accomplish that goal
5. A quick and specific action plan

A template of this Mission Statement is provided in your Dare Action Plan.

When I wrote my first mission statement in that format, it was very money-oriented and it took me a few months to comprehend why I wasn't motivated. I then wrote a goal-oriented/dream statement and that turned out to be the first step in my writing this book.

You can make it simpler and follow the format Simon Sinek suggests in *Find Your Why*:

"To (*contribution*), so that (*impact*)"

In other words, what are you willing to do, how do you want to contribute to your family's happiness, to your community, to the environment *so* you have a positive impact on those important areas in your life?

He advises that there is no such thing as separate personal and professional mission statements; instead, they should be put into one mission statement given that you're one human being trying to align your actions in order to achieve one big goal, something you feel is bigger than yourself.

Just to better illustrate, here is a sample mission statement:

"To share my knowledge so we can build a better country."

Vision or Dreams boards are another way of drafting a mission statement. I first heard of them three years ago while browsing the internet. Simply put, it's a visual representation of your dreams and goals, a way to take them out of your head and onto a piece of paper. You can be creative and do this any way you like. You can adopt a "bucket list" format, draw whatever you feel relates to your dreams, or print out images that are meaningful to you.

I believe it goes without saying that you have to put your 2D manifestation of your dreams on a board or even a wall for it to become a real "vision board."

The format you give your mission statement doesn't matter. The important thing is that you have one and you see it every single day so you make your dream a reality. Read it out loud every day. Incorporate reading it into your daily routine whether it's after brushing your teeth or first thing when you wake up in the morning.

When you define your mission, it's very important that you consider a few things:

1. **Your goal must be clear, actionable, and precise.** Let's suppose you want to become a freelance travel writer. That is a broad and vague statement that doesn't necessarily define your job. Instead, say what it means to be a travel writer (e.g., writing four hours a day, pitching to prospective clients one hour per day and travelling).

2. **Set a time to work on your goal, *every single day*.** You have to be consistent in order to achieve your goal. Say that, to be a freelance travel writer, you write every day from 7 a.m.–12 p.m. and you travel the last week of every month.

3. **Break every big goal into small tasks.** In order to succeed as a freelance travel writer, you'll have to prepare samples, draft a portfolio, research prospective clients, send pitches, etc. If you break preparing samples into gathering what you have written, making a list of ideas to add, grouping them into similar themes, and writing two samples a day, you'll finish this task before you know it.

4. **Give yourself a deadline for each small step.** Don't let yourself drag out your to-do list forever. Set a deadline and do your best to meet it.

5. **Celebrate the small victories.** I know it's easy to forget to give yourself a pat on the back every time you achieve something, but it's important. Have a list of things worth celebrating (big and small) and check it at the end of each week. Reward yourself for what you have accomplished.

Keep in mind . . .

- If you write down who you are, you will never forget.
- A mission is a job only the brave are willing to undertake.
- Consistency is the name of the game.

CHAPTER 5

Organize your finances

At this point, having stated what you're willing to give to the world and how you intend to do so, it's time to ask: Do I have enough money to afford this change?

No one can deny the importance of financial preparation when plotting the course of their life.

Prepare your freedom fund, if you don't have one already

A freedom fund is the savings you put aside to give you freedom of choice in the future.

It's a percentage of your earnings that you let just sit there for emergencies, — such as being fired, breaking an arm, or changing jobs. Some might call it an "emergency fund," but I like "freedom fund" because it gives you the freedom not to panic over future events. With a freedom fund, you can figure out your next move, without depending on anybody else.

That is different from what I call the "fun fund," which will serve to sponsor your dream trip, to buy your partner's birthday present, or even to pay someone to do grocery shopping for you (believe me, lazy days *are real*!).

But back to the freedom fund, as soon as your salary comes into your account, put a percentage of it in a hard-to-access account. From your income, you should allocate a certain percentage to your main bills (rent, food, utilities, etc.), another to have fun and treat yourself to a hairstylist (yes, you deserve it!), and the third part to your savings.

Many experts believe that 20 percent is a good amount to save every month. However, if 20 percent is unrealistic for you, a simple quick way to start saving money without feeling like you have to make huge sacrifices would be what I'm calling *pocket money savings*, which is no new concept. Basically, all you have to do is take the money in your pockets and save it somewhere, as soon as you get home each day.

My partner tested this out for three months straight, without missing a day, and managed to save over 18,000 Kz (approximately $50 USD). It may not sound like a lot of money but think of what you would have bought with it versus how much value $50 US dollars can add to your life if you multiply it.

If you're not the keep-money-in-the-pocket kind of person, just take the lowest value bill or the coins in your wallet and drop it in the savings jar. The idea here is to work on your saving mindset so you start learning how to make money serve you in a more efficient way.

If you don't control your money, it will control you and you'll never be in charge of your life. Remember: money is a great servant, but a dreadful master.

Another option would be to get an investor or a loan. Borrowing money is an extremely sensitive matter because you'll be using somebody else's money for <u>your</u> benefit/project and that will put extra pressure on you. Nonetheless, if you truly believe your new career is worth the risk, study this carefully and make your decision.

If you decide to ask for a loan, consider the following:

1. Will you ask a friend, family member, or a financial institution?

2. If you go for the family or friend option, that will have an effect on your relationship, especially in case things go wrong. That is, if you're not capable to pay on time or if you cannot pay them back at all. Reflect on how you'd handle the situation and if it's worth the risk.

3. If you ask a family member or friend, go for someone who is financially comfortable so that it doesn't put them in a tenuous position.

4. If you decide to go for financial institutions, watch out for interest rates. Take the time to evaluate if the interest rates are favorable, and be realistic in terms of being able to keep up with the payments.

5. In both cases, if you fail to follow the agreement to the letter, you risk tainting your reputation as a debtor, ultimately compromising your future ability to get credit.

6. Go for people/institutions that are reputable and may offer you guidance and/or consulting.

7. Realize that a loan will affect your cash flow. That means that on the top of the expenses you have, you also will have to include the loan payments with interest.

8. You may lose freedom with business decisions since you have to report all your activities periodically, and it's expected they are perfectly aligned with your initial business plan.

9. Decide if a lawyer is necessary. Depending on the entity you deal with and the kind of written agreement in question, you may need one to make sure you understand all the details. However, most financial institutions have personnel available to answer all your questions and facilitate the process. My advice: always have a written settlement, signed by both parties, regardless of whom you get your loan from.

Have a monthly budget and stick to it

Yes, a budget! There are countless apps and tools that can help you control and stick to your budget, including a Microsoft Excel template, which will help you establish a personal and family budget.

The main features I appreciate in this type of tool are:

— Projected and Actual Monthly Income: this one is useful if you have multiple sources of income. It's also useful for you to be realistic about what your average income is.

— Different sections such as housing, entertainment, transportation, loans, taxes, food, and personal care. The most important ones for me are "savings" and "investments" so I can track those categories.

— A visual of my income, expenses, and savings in the form of a graph or diagram.

For you to truly see how you spend your money, enter each expenditure in an app or even an excel sheet every single time money is going out. I know, it's boring and sounds obsessive, but it's to protect you from a financial disaster.

Once you start budgeting, I encourage you to look into your budget tracking tool once a month to identify where your money's going and identify areas where you can reduce costs and direct your money elsewhere.

Ever since I started monitoring my budget, I became much better at controlling my expenses and for that, I don't need to control them so tightly anymore, because I just spend money on what I know is worth it, and yes, that does include a ridiculously freezing Cuca (Angolan beer) twice a week.

If you're in a relationship with shared finances or have a family, I recommend you hold monthly meetings, just to check your progress toward your financial goal.

Reduce expenses

Now that you know what you're spending your money on, do you really need to get your nails done once a week? What about that top you bought that you will never wear?

When I went freelancing and knew that my monthly earnings wouldn't be the same or even regular, for a while, I instantly knew I had to be much smarter with my spendings and money allocation.

Like a magic trick of the universe, I stumbled upon a video about minimalism: just having the essentials. That got me into decluttering and automatically buying less, which ultimately made me a better consumer.

I'm not saying you should become a minimalist but start thinking about what you really need in your life, from material possessions to personal and professional relationships. Maybe you'll realize you don't need to pay for an event to have fun or that you can treat yourself to a manicure session at home with the bonus of watching that movie you've been meaning to watch forever.

You can also find small jobs that pay for your fun activities, — such as being a food critic (everybody needs to eat), amusement park tester, or product reviewer. The sky is the limit! This way, you keep having a blast and discover new ways of generating money by being happy. For links of fun jobs, please check the resources page on my blog https://pessimainfeliz.com/resources/.

Exchanging or borrowing things instead of buying can also be an alternative. Join one of those "buy nothing groups" and you can exchange the most surprising items. You can create one yourself using social media. As you see, reducing your expenses doesn't have to be painful.

But before you start cutting off costs, it's important you identify where you need to do so, without feeling like you're losing a limb. Remember the different sections I told you about in a budgeting app? Well, choose the easiest one for you to stop spending money on. If you have a family, you might want to start from the category that least benefits your loved ones, like sweets in the food section or hairdresser every week in the beauty section.

In practice, let's say you've been monitoring your "entertainment" section for a month:

— Movies with snacks: $60 USD

— Drinks: $45 USD

— Concerts: $180 USD

— Netflix subscription: $16 USD

If my entertainment section looked like the one above, I would start by reducing the frequency rather than scratching the activity from my list altogether. For instance, if I went to the movies less often, I could still keep my Netflix subscription or if I reduced my alcohol intake, I could enjoy healthier and cheaper drinks, while saving some money. The main purpose is for you to get awareness and control over your spending habits.

You can often reduce costs while being social as well. There is often power in numbers whether it is a potluck picnic, buying in bulk and sharing, or splitting the cost of a vacation house. Reducing expenses can revive a sense of community and even strengthen relationships.

Keep in mind . . .

- Saving small will pay off big.
- See budgeting as a money game, not as a social constraint.
- Remember, the best things in life are free (or very cheap, anyway)!

From the Outside In

CHAPTER 6

Do your research

Having that deep money talk with yourself and looking at the numbers is one of the most important steps toward your freedom. Now, take your eyes off the page and look around. How are others doing what you want to do? How might this career change affect your life? What tools will you need?

Get in touch with the pros and get your hands dirty

There's nothing better than talking to someone who's been where you're heading and finding out what they did well, and also where they screwed up (we all like the juicy details).

When I wanted to become a translator and interpreter, I told everyone that I was providing those services. I even got an interpreting job at a conference, where I offered to work for free and told them I had no experience. They accepted and the day of the conference I was beyond nervous. Head pounding and hands sweating, I made it through, and in the end, they decided to pay me as a professional. I got the business card of a translation services agency and even managed to talk to a professional translator to ask all the questions I could.

Try to go to events where you know professionals in your sector will be, ask friends and family if they know someone who has that certain job, go on LinkedIn and offer them a soda to talk (although you might have better luck if you offer a beer), stop them in an event to introduce yourself and talk. If you come across them, don't be afraid of asking questions. Just don't forget to be polite and use your genuine charm.

Educate and develop yourself

Somehow, I had embedded in me this misconception that once you're done with university, most of your learning in life is over. No more tests to pass, no more exams to take, no more sleepless nights finishing assignments. If only I knew!

Learning is, or at least should be, a never-ending process in everybody's life, especially when you decide to take control over all areas of your life. Therefore, before you quit your job, and even after, make sure you educate yourself as much as you can. Nowadays, you can have access to virtually any type of material on any kind of topic.

Read books, listen to TED talks, go to free events to share ideas, mingle with different people, talk to strangers. You'd be amazed with how much you can absorb from a stranger's small talk in an elevator. Don't forget to book time daily for your own education!

Also, check if your new job will require you to have a certification or attend a certain training course. At the beginning you may not need it, as you figure out your niche, style and professional needs, but set higher learning goals and work toward them.

While you're at it, remember to develop your people skills. Be naturally pleasant and seek to see the best in others, by treating them with respect and kindness. Empathy should be your new surname and not just a label. David Parnell, author and co-founder of *The Legal Institute for Forward Thinking and Forbes contributor,* defines it in the following way: "People skills are, in short, the various attributes and competencies that allow one to play well with others." You can find fun ways to communicate and innovate in a manner to show that you care about everyone you work with: customers, partners, suppliers, etc.

Later in chapter 12, in customer retention, I give you tips on how to put your people skills into practice and genuinely develop healthy and solid professional relationships by using your charismatic abilities.

Keep in mind . . .

- You don't need to reinvent the wheel, just give a call to an inventor.

- "Education is the most powerful weapon which you can use to change the world." Nelson Mandela.

- Being "likeable" *is* a learnable skill.

CHAPTER 7

Have an accountability partner and hold yourself accountable as well

Talk your mission statement and goals through with your closest people. If you're in a relationship, speak honestly about how this will affect you financially and study the scenarios.

You can also choose to have someone else hold you accountable as you start working toward your goals. It can be someone senior, who will also provide you with some guidance and a parental "it-will-be-OK" kind of support. You have to make it on your own, but you don't have to be alone.

Don't forget to take responsibility for your own decisions and actions. Keep yourself on track and make your accountability partner proud. Celebrate private victories before making them public.

For that, you have to "show up every day" by accomplishing those mini-goals that lead you to the big one. If working on your business plan is your first step, break it down into small simple and tangible tasks, such as:

1. Set a deadline for having the whole plan complete and deadlines for each section of the business plan
2. Write down each part of the plan to be completed
3. Set a time schedule in your calendar to work on each part
4. Set a minimum amount you have to get done every day
5. Communicate your action plan to your accountability partner

This way, you'll have to regularly check with your accountability partner, which will help you stay on track.

Keep in mind . . .

- Accountability will make you feel safer and responsibility will make you feel stronger.
- Show up every day; this is how you make your way.

CHAPTER 8

Design your business plan

Once you've done your research and spoken to your accountability partner, you'll have a more realistic idea about your wish of becoming a freelancer, especially after looking at your bank account. So now with that knowledge, you need to try to plan ahead and have a sort of brain dump session, where you take your idea from your head to paper.

A business plan is a detailed layout of your business structure, which helps you think about its different areas and manage expectations.

In general, your business plan should cover these areas:

— **Business identity**: Name, mission, vision, and values

— **Products and services**: What are you selling and which problem does it solve?

— **Target audience**: Who are your customers?

— **Market research**: How's the current business sector? What do customers want? What is missing? Who are your competitors?

- **Marketing strategy**: Why are you choosing methods *XYZ* to promote your business? What's your strategic growth plan?

- **Operations and logistics**: How's your production going to work? Which delivery methods will you use? Will you need suppliers?

- **Financial plan**: What is going to be your cost and pricing strategy? What are your financial forecasts? Do you have a business budget?

- **Legal and accounting aspects**: How to legitimize your activity and have no problems with taxes (specifically for US freelancers)? How do you know when to handle those areas?

In this chapter, I will go into more detail in each part of the business and how you can structure them.

Business Identity

First of all, how do you want people to know you? What's the name you want them to associate your products and services with? As a freelancer, it's totally acceptable to simply make this your name. But if you choose to create a "business persona," make sure the name is no more than three words long and speaks to your personality. Your friends and family should be able to say it's you because it sounds and feels like the person they know.

If you use a tagline, make sure it's straight forward and says exactly what you do, such as "John Baker Photography — Making your wedding photos feel timeless."

It is important to differentiate mission, vision, and values. Your mission is about why you do what you do. How you want to change the world for the better.

Your vision is what you want to have accomplished in the future. This can be very ambitious, such as:

— AIESEC's vision: "Peace and the fulfillment of humankind's potential."

— Netflix vision statement: "To continue being one of the leading firms of the internet entertainment era."

— Google vision statement: "To provide access to the world's information in one click."

Values are basically your beliefs and behaviour in order to live up to your mission and vision. Think of them as the action steps to achieve your final goal. Uber has done a beautiful job defining its values, for instance:

— We build globally, we live locally.

— We are customer obsessed.

— We celebrate differences.

— We do the right thing. Period.

— We act like owners.

— We persevere.

— We value ideas over hierarchy.

— We make big bold bets.

Products and services

It's essential that you know exactly what you're selling and make sure you master it until you diversify or expand somehow. Which problems would your products or service be solving?

I remember ignoring an experienced interpreter's advice to only work in one pair of languages. I still tried to work in two and noticed it was preventing me from evolving at all. As soon as I understood and followed his advice, the improvements were palpable.

When working as a content writer, I evolved exponentially because I focused my attention on one kind of topic and the same content creation technique. Today, I can write articles about the gastronomic and hotel market almost with my eyes closed.

And the main problem I'm solving, you ask? Lack of information about the Angolan food and tourism sector.

Know what it is you are offering and immerse yourself in that world. Find ways to add value and solve people's problems. Be the person you wish you could hire. Don't try to be everything to everyone. Specialize and find your niche so you can be great at that one thing.

Define your target audience

Identify who would buy your products/services so you can figure out which kind of person they would be and think like a potential customer. To do that, draft the profile of your prospect avatar. (If you don't yet know who your target customer is you may want to do some market research first to help you decide.)

Here are the questions that may help you build your avatar:

- What is their name, age, occupation, and education level?
- What are five character traits they possess?
- What are their three biggest fears?
- What are their three main hobbies?
- What are the three main frustrations they are dealing with?
- What's their social status and income?
- What are their goals?
- What do they like and dislike? (three items for each)
- Where are they hanging out?
- What are they watching and reading?
- How do they communicate with the world?

— Where do they work? (industry, sector, location)

— What do they want to avoid/eliminate from their life?

When you draft your prospect avatar, do it as if you were putting a resume together for that person, with a picture as well, if that helps. Then put yourself in their position, and try figuring out how you could reach them and make them want your product.

At this point, if possible, start compiling contact details of potential customers you might have access to, for your mailing list. Building up a mailing list will stretch your reach by a mile and marketing to people you've interacted with will be the icing on the cake.

However, be careful to not email too often. It makes you look desperate and less professional.

For avatar templates, please go to the resources page of my blog https://pessimainfeliz.com/resources/.

Do market research

Once you know who you want to reach, conducting market research is the next step. You probably are not in the position of spending any money on market research or extra tools, at this point, but luckily for you, there are plenty of market research tools you can use for free, at the beginning of your freelancing career. Here are a few of them:

— **Google trends**: this tool allows you to track which keywords are popular, where in the world and its fluctuation in popularity over the last years. That is, if you want to know where your target clients are, you can see it on the charts, maps, and graphs the site shows. Additionally, you can compare keywords to see which terms are more popular.

You will find a more comprehensive guide on how to use google trends to find your niche on the resources page (https://pessimainfeliz.com/resources/), but here are a few of the amazing features the site has:

1. Geo search: you can choose the country you want to search for as soon as you land on the website

2. Search popularity over time: you can choose to see for the past 12 months, past hour, or even customize your time limit

3. Maps with interest by region, subregion, and even city

4. Top five related topics: the keywords/terms searched by the same users who searched for your keyword

5. Top five related queries: the searched queries related to your keywords, searched by the same users

— **Facebook Audience Insights:** for this one, you need a Facebook business page (which is free), and then you'll have access to information about your followers and

Facebook users in general so you can find more potential followers and create content that interests them.

— **Google Alerts:** this one basically is future-oriented. When you insert a search term and set it up to be monitored, google alerts will send you emails whenever it finds online content with your search term, including web pages, blogs, and even YouTube. This way you can know when your search term is used and where and adjust your business strategy accordingly.

— **Market Research Survey:** The thing about market surveys is that if you are at the very beginning, likely your mailing list is not too large and that may not give you a significant sample. Nonetheless, you can still make the most of the suggestions people make through the survey to position yourself or test out suggested products.

You should know that with these free market research survey services you cannot send the survey to more than 100 to 250 participants and on some of them you get a few suggested questions to improve your feedback. Here are a few of the most popular:

— SoGoSurvey

— Survey Monkey

— Google Forms

— Survey Planet

Once you've gathered all that information, don't forget to take note of the key findings, to look at them closely, and to identify the business opportunities.

Define your marketing strategy

People can't buy what they don't know about. With this in mind, I suggest you conduct a SWOT analysis (strengths, weaknesses, opportunities, and threats) of your business to identify the opportunities to make it more visible and accessible. This way, you'll make it easier to see what your USP (unique selling point) is and outline it to your audience. Also, once you have all those areas well spotted, you can work on your growth plan.

Here are the main parts of your marketing strategy:

SWOT analysis

To conduct your SWOT analysis, ask these questions:

Strengths

- What do you do exceptionally well?
- What are the positive aspects of your product?
- What makes you and your product/service better than the others on the market?

Weaknesses

- What lets your business down?

- What are your blind spots?

- What are your limitations?

Opportunities

- What gaps are in the market that your product/service may fill in?

- Are there new openings in the market?

- Which resources are already available?

Threats

- Which factors could harm your business?

- How's your current professional reputation?

- How is the competition doing?

Here is an example of a SWOT analysis for a freelancer:

Strengths

- Your strategic location

- Time flexibility

- Specialized in a skill

- Unique selling point

Weaknesses

- No name in the market yet

- No client list yet

- Limited in the services you can offer in some way

- Lack of resources

Opportunities

- New demand for your specific product/service

- Your competitors' vulnerabilities

- Seasonal celebrations

- Economic situation

Threats

- Competitors' advantages

- Lack of training

- High cost of equipment

Promotional strategy

From that analysis, you can decide which one will be the best promotional strategy for you:

- **Advertising in traditional media** (radio, TV, magazines, etc.)

- **Personal selling** (in person or via phone)

- **Short-term promotions** (offer your products/services with a discount or even for free)

- **Direct marketing** (send letters, emails, or brochures to individual target customer)

- **Online marketing** (using social media and creating online presence)

You can actually choose a couple of those strategies to help you. For instance, I began with direct marketing because I was aiming for high paying customers and was confident enough in my skills. But I also use online marketing consistently, and in my first interactions with my first group of customers, I used short-term promotions.

If you choose social media as your main marketing tool, since it may feel it's the most cost-efficient, don't think you have to be everywhere at once. Start from the social media account you're already familiar with, master it, and only then add in the next one. After a month or two, check the analytics to see where your traffic is coming from or where most of your clients have heard of your services.

You can also always count on your friends help to spot potential new customers. Don't forget that word of mouth is still a great form of marketing and doing an excellent job will encourage everyone to share the word.

Growth strategy plan

While there are hundreds of ways you could choose to design your growth strategy, I'm going to suggest the model produced by the work of Igor Ansoff, the "father of strategic management," according to *The Economist*, that illustrates the four principal strategies a business can apply to attain long-term growth:

A. **Market Penetration:** selling more products/services to the same customers, that is, your target market.

B. **Market Development:** selling the same products/services to a different market or customer segment.

C. **Product Development:** selling new products/services to the same target market.

D. **Diversification:** selling new products/services to different markets.

Keep in mind that as the strategies change from *A* to *D*, the risk gets higher, meaning that your chances of success are higher if you bet on market penetration than if you decide to diversify.

Nonetheless, all of the strategies are possible and can be sustainable if implemented correctly. I recommend you research each of them and choose the one you see yourself being successful applying. Know that, as you grow, your growth strategy may change as well so no need to agonize over this. Yet, it's important to have a plan and give yourself time to work on it until you feel it should change.

Operations and logistics

When planning for your systems and processes, you need to know how the product is getting to the end customer and also how are you getting paid. Creating easy communication channels is also advisable.

Processes and Procedures

Standardize as many of your processes and procedures as you can, from the first interaction with a prospective customer to the moment you're getting paid. By that, I mean written documents or templates that will speed up your response rate.

Let's suppose you're a freelance writer who's pitching for *Forbes*. You send your pitch and after a week, you follow up. A few days later you finally get a positive response, you exchange a few emails with the editor to align everything, and you deliver the final draft two days later. It's time for payment, so you send the invoice and wait until the end of the month to receive it.

From the example above, there are at least five templates you should have ready:

1. The initial pitch template

This is one of the most important documents for a freelancer because it's your first impression to a prospective client. A simple guide I use to draft one is:

Subject: What the client has asked on its guidelines or "pitch-my offer" (e.g., Pitch — Article about Angolan traditional food)

Main body: follow the given template or start by praising them for their work, give a 50 to 80-word summary of the professional accomplishments relevant to the pitch, guide them to relevant links (your portfolio, website, and relevant publications), and give a rough structure of the proposed article. Avoid attachments unless otherwise requested.

2. The follow-up email

I advise you send this email 7 to 10 days after the first one so it's not too nagging and you still show interest and professionalism. Keep it short and to the point, yet friendly.

E.g., *"Hi Name/ dear sir/madam, I'd like to know if you are interested in the pitch I sent below. Thank you for your time."*

3. First interaction response

This will probably vary, depending on the client and the service provided, but basically, this is a set of questions you should prepare once the client shows interest in working with you. I go into depth about it in chapter 13.

4. Invoice template

5. Follow-up email in case you're not paid on time

Keep the tone friendly but firm

E.g., *" Hi Name, I'm writing because I haven't received the payment for job X yet and was wondering if there is any issue I'm not aware of. Please let me know if there's anything I can do to help."*

Those are only the documents for that particular interaction, but you should prepare a few for the most common activities in your business, such as Professional Bio, Business presentation, Confidentiality Agreement and so on.

Payment methods

Which payment methods will you want to have? How are you preventing clients from not paying you?

When I started offering my translation services, signing up on freelance websites, such as Upwork, helped me a great deal. It is quite competitive, but don't let that frustrate you. Nonetheless, most of those websites have a safe payment system that will protect you from bad customers.

But in the case of clients you deal with directly, think about how you will want to deal with delayed payments. Requiring a deposit upfront may be an option but remember you're a beginner so be very cautious if you choose this method, since you can be easily replaced.

What I'd advise you to do here is to try to find out who your customer is and see who's worked for them before. If you use the freelance websites, you'll have that information on the reviews provided by fellow freelancers. Do your research.

As for payment methods, most clients are comfortable using PayPal, which currently takes 2.9% + $0.30 per transaction and has no setup or monthly fees, but I have used bank transfer as well and have never had a problem with it. There are quite a few options regarding online payment, such as:

— **Google Checkout:** fees start at 2.9% + $0.30 per transaction for sales less than $3,000. The percentage they take goes down depending on monthly sales volume.

— **Amazon Payments:** fees start at 2.9% + $0.30 per transaction for payments over $10 (the percentage they take is less for larger transactions). For payments under $10, the fee is 5.0% + $0.05 per transaction.

— **Dwolla:** no fees for transactions less than $10. For transactions over $10, Dwolla charges $0.25 per transaction.

In my experience, 98 percent of customers are honest and nice, as long as you keep communication clear and deliver what you promised. Don't waste much time with the remaining two percent. Trust your gut and don't do business with them.

Financial plan

In chapter five, we talked about organizing your finances and making a budget. Now, you need to do the same, but specifically for your business. For that, I recommend you separate your personal accounts from your business ones, just for clarity, organization, and ease for the accountant.

The following are the essential parts of a financial plan. You may add or delete the parts as it suits your business.

Cost and pricing strategy

Start from defining how much you want/can spend on the initial investment and design a strategy for that. For instance, let's say you have $5000 USD to start your photography freelance business. You need to decide if you're spending everything in equipment, or if you're allocating part of the money to each area (marketing, market research, etc.) and how much would that be.

Then, define your pricing strategy. Will you position yourself as a low-, mid-, or high-price product/service provider? I go a bit more into depth later in chapter 15 of part two of this book, but you'll need to decide beforehand which price tag you want to stamp on your products/services and draft a plan to test the demand and acceptance.

Financial forecast

Use the above information, as well as the market research details, to estimate your future sales and costs, and feel free to make a few assumptions about the market trends, since seasonal commercial tendencies often have a big impact on them.

Also, remember to define a financial goal. Be that monthly, quarterly or annual.

Business budget

Similar to your personal budget allocation, you'll need to estimate your current business costs. If you're a stay-at-home freelancer, it's easy to ignore costs such as internet, electricity, water, and telephone, since they are already part of your personal budget.

However, if you pay attention, especially if you live with somebody else, those costs can easily go higher and have a long-term impact on your finances in general. Therefore, even if you're not going to separate those from your personal expenses, at least acknowledge them so you don't have any surprises and can monitor the changes.

That will help you identify opportunities to reduce costs and what elements you should take into account for your growth strategy.

Legal and aspects of the business

This is probably one of the most pertinent questions future freelancers ask. While I won't be able to give you a specific answer, since this is very particular to each country, here are a few steps to take to get the information you need:

1. Have your business plan very clearly defined so you can identify which kind of entity you are

2. Decide if you want your business to have your name or its own. That implies a few changes in the legal status

3. Find out which competent authority regulates your activity and do some preliminary research on them. You can probably get that information from your country's labor legislation or your government website

4. Consult an accountant and/or a lawyer to guide you through the process and tell you which is the best way to pay taxes and avoid unnecessary charges

If you're an American freelancer, I recommend you read *Make Money as a Freelance Writer* by Gina Horney and Sally Miller, where they give the step by step guide of how to legalize your freelance activity.

Keep in mind . . .

- Creating a business image is the equivalent of an identification document for your practice. Take it seriously and make it memorable.

- Think of your products/services as a problem-solver.

- Your target audience is key to the development of your business. Take the time to know who they are.

- Market research gives you perspective.

- Think long term and adjust your strategy as you evolve.

- Make your processes and procedures a "do with my eyes shut" game to maximize efficiency.

- Put the numbers on paper because they will be the evidence of the performance of your business.

- Get the legal and accounting part sorted ASAP, preferably by a professional.

CHAPTER 9

Do a test-drive

Congratulations on completing your rough draft business plan. This is a crucial step that of gives you a more realistic idea of how things will or should run in your business and life. And now, it's time to run a test-drive on what you envision as your new career routine.

Set a work schedule for freelancing while you have a conventional job

Setting some time aside to do extra work may be the last thing you want to do, especially if you have to wake up early just to sit in hours of traffic to get to work, but remember this is a temporary test for you to not have to face that kind of traffic ever again.

Two to four hours a day should be enough for you to focus on your now side hustle, soon to be your full-time job. Try to be very focused on the core activity. At this stage, knowing and developing the main product is the only priority.

Grab every opportunity you can to work on your project and prove your worth. If you want to make a career out of painting, paint something for your colleagues or neighbours. I'm not saying friends and family because they tend to say something nice so as to not hurt your feelings, which is sweet, but you won't survive on sweetness alone.

Ask that person if they'd pay for that product/service and how much they'd be willing to spend. At work, if you have an opportunity to spend some time doing what you want to do as a freelancer, go for it! In fact, it was by volunteering to translate a few documents at work that I discovered my way out of the corporate world.

Use your vacation time to experience what your life would be like as a freelancer

I know you want to "chillax" during your holidays and not think about work at all. But, please bear with me! You can set up a few freelance gigs to work on over your vacation so you can get a feel for what that life may be like. You may discover that you'll spend many hours of emailing back and forth with clients that you will need to account for, have numerous phone calls you'll have to find a quiet place for, have trouble getting supplies that will have to be purchased in advance. Your vacation time offers you a low-risk way of working out the kinks, and a chance to see if you think the reality of freelancing is really for you. Are you able to start work at eight and work all day without distractions if there's no boss to report to?

The Angolan law allows up to 22 days of holidays per year. The company I worked for allowed me to take all 22 days at once so I worked as a freelancer during that time. I found it worked for me, and when I got back to work, I gave my 30-day notice resignation letter. Check out your company's regulations to see if you could do something similar.

Consider providing services for free as a test

By doing some work for free, you are getting some exposure and are able to focus on the service you will offer, without the added pressure of being dependant on the income. You will give yourself a chance to develop your skills.

When I decided to work as a freelance translator, I would take every translation job I could get my hands on so I could measure my capabilities and delivery capacity. I managed to roughly figure out how many words I could translate in an hour and in a day, learned what the best work environment was for me, determined what documents to avoid (too technical and required more research than I could handle), which preliminary questions to ask before taking a job. I also asked for feedback all the time and identified some new potential customers in the process.

You can see the benefits of forgetting about the money for a while and focusing on the learning curve. Even if you decide to freelance in a sector or industry you have solid experience in, remember there will be aspects of freelancing that you're probably not familiar with. Maybe you just know the product, but you don't know how to deal with customers directly. Grab every chance to practice you have!

Keep in mind . . .

- Make the most of your trial run, while you still have a day job. That will keep your feet on the ground while you get a taste of your dream.

- Make sure you constantly evaluate your performance. Don't take on more work than you can do well while also working at your current job.

- While you can, drop the price tag and focus on the experience.

CHAPTER 10

Do not close doors behind you

Practicing your gig as a side hustle before making it a full-time job will build up your confidence and client base, and eventually lead you to make the decision to leave your traditional job. If you do leave your place of work, remember that quitting a job is very similar to breaking up with a romantic partner. It requires maturity, understanding, and kindness. Do it with all those qualities in mind.

Consider the part-time option

If after your trial run you find freelancing a good fit, you may want to reduce your work hours to part time while you build up your client base and reputation in your new field. It can be a good idea to cut back your work hours gradually instead of quitting altogether. If working part time is not an option, you could consider leaving that job and taking another half-day job to allow you to still have a steady income but dedicate more time to freelancing.

When it's time to leave your job, do so with integrity

Say goodbye with an open smile and light spirit.

When I left my company, the whole last month was quite emotional. My manager was determined to change my mind, so she set up meetings with the executive board. The process confirmed for me what I wanted to do and why I had to leave. It made things clear to me and gave me peace of mind. In the end, I left with positivity on both sides, there were no hard feelings.

Leave in a way you know you could come back if you wanted to and the conditions allowed.

If you have already flown into freelance land without following any of those steps, don't worry, you still have salvation. I wish I followed all those steps before I started freelancing. My journey started with many blind areas, just playing with instinct and luck. If you have not prepared for this leap of faith in managing your own career, don't panic as you were smart enough to read this book.

Keep in mind . . .

- Leave a legacy of kindness and professionalism when you quit your job.
- If you haven't done so, it's never too late to make amends.

PART II

I Took the Jump, What Now?

"The only really committed artist is he who, without refusing to take part in the combat, at least refuses to join the regular armies and remains a freelance."

—Albert Camus

When you look things from up close, they gain space in reality and loose room in dreamland. At this point, you've gone through the process of thinking about being a freelancer to actually doing it.

This part of the book will give you the ABC's of freelancing in the real world, providing you tips on how to set everything up mentally and physically for you to begin, the whole package about clients, from how to find them to customer retention, your work methodology all the way to time management.

The fear of freelancing is a subject that is not addressed enough and here I share with you the techniques I still use to deal with them and the effect they have on me.

CHAPTER 11

Set your goals, schedule, and workspace

Having prepared for this moment and now living it, where do you begin? How to prepare for this new chapter?

What is your goal?

As Stephen Covey would advise you, "Start with the end in mind." That simply means that you need to know where you're going in order to take the most effective steps in the right direction. Visualize your destination and define the steps you're taking to get there.

To do that, ask questions: Where do you want to go? What's your main achievement? How long do you want to take to get there? What are your milestones?

That can be a fun way of defining and visualizing your goals. Personally, I follow the format suggested by Napoleon Hill in *Think and Grow Rich* where I set a maximum of three goals per category:

— Personal development

— Health

- Family and relationships

- Financial

- Professional

- Community

You can also create or eliminate categories to make this vision board fully yours and identify what's most important for you.

The next step is to identify your three main challenges or concerns, your three main strengths, and finally the top priorities from the above list, those three things that you believe will have the biggest impact in your life and in the lives of your loved ones. Last but not least, design an action plan for each of your goals. How will you make these a reality?

Do not make the mistake of setting too many goals. Ten main goals a year should be enough. That is, for some categories you may have just one main goal, while for others you may feel the need to have more. What you have to do next is break those goals down into actionable steps, because that's how you eat an elephant, one bite at a time.

To give you a solid example, let's say that on January 1, 2020, you define your three big goals in the professional category:

1. Become a freelancer by June 30, 2020

Step 1: Decide what will be your freelancing activity by January 15

Step 2: Finish your business plan by April 15

Step 3: Start offering services by April 16

2. Strengthen my professional relationships

Step 1: Make a list of coworkers' birthdays by January 10 and prepare a personalized message to send them on the day

Step 2: Attend at least one professional event per month

Step 3: Find one or two professional groups (Facebook or forums) in my sector and interact in the group at least once a week

3. Expand my knowledge and training

Do research and draft a list of courses you want to take by April 15

Get a certification/attend a training course specific to your sector by May 15

Read one book a month on my sector

Notice that the set deadline for each goal and step so you can align your activities chronologically. That will help you hold yourself accountable and be realistic about working toward your goals. You can always adjust things if circumstances change, but don't delay a deadline just because you were lazy.

The list of strengths and weaknesses can be a general one that covers all areas, but you can also do one for each category, depending on its importance. For instance, that list for the professional category could look something like this:

Strengths

— I'm great with people

— I have good organizing skills

— Commitment is my surname!

Weaknesses

— Poor time management

— Can't deal with finances

— Lack of consistency

The trick here is for you to leverage your strengths and work on your weaknesses so they don't get in the way. A pro tip is to capitalize on your strengths and ask for help to tackle the weak spots. Your accountability partner definitely could lend you a hand for this task.

Jump quickly to your most important goals, the ones that you believe will change your life, picking those from the categories closer to your dream, and you don't have to choose three, one should do.

Last year, I chose the goal of reading 24 books. That was because I knew that being closer to books would not only teach me a great deal but would also motivate me to write this one, which was something I wanted to do for the longest time. Do you think it changed my life? The answer to that will be a whole new book.

Remember, your goal setting scheme doesn't have to be rigid. You're allowed to change it as you learn and grow from your experiences. After all, the final goal here is for you to know where you're headed. If it so happens that you changed your mind about going to a sunny beach and now prefer a snowy location, so be it. Enjoy the journey and have fun.

"Goodbye 9–5" — That's a myth!

For at least a year after becoming a freelancer, I made the mistake of not having a set schedule and would brag about working whenever I wanted to. As a freelancer, the saying "time is money" will take on a new meaning for you.

Because you can work as little or as much as you want, you'll notice that, in the beginning, you'll either neglect and underestimate the amount of work you have or you'll exhaust yourself, working easily 12–14 hours a day.

Even if it feels like there's no other way to do it at the beginning, just because you're trying to figure everything out, give yourself a deadline. Let's say you give yourself three weeks to work overtime. I'm not saying you'll have everything figured out by then (because you never will), but at least you'll know much more than when you started and that will allow you to make smarter mistakes and avoid past ones.

After that initial stage, define a "normal" working time and try to stick to it. If you work the conventional 9–5-time window, you'll have time for the other areas of your life, and you won't feel as if you're missing out on life itself. Otherwise, chances are, when your friends leave work and invite you to hang out and unwind after a long day of work, you'll feel tempted to follow them and tell yourself you can always work till dawn. Hate to break it to you, but your motivation and energy levels will most likely be less than what's needed to focus on work.

Have a well-organized schedule and stick to it

Speaking of working hours, you'll need an organized schedule to know what you're doing next. Whether you prefer a digital or paper agenda, it's crucial that you have one.

What works for me is using an app such as *Microsoft To Do* to list out everything I have to do. This is an app that allows you to have different lists (e.g., personal tasks, professional activities, or errands), and you can have folders and sub-tasks inside the main ones. You can set reminders and deadlines for each task. It's quite organized and has many useful functions.

There are a number of similar apps and they are getting better by the hour. Just choose the one that works for you and get your tasks out of your head.

After I have planned out my list, I allocate each task to a time slot in my calendar (in some apps, you can just synchronize your to-do list with your calendar, to make it easier and then adjust at your convenience.) and do the following:

1. Color code different types of activity (e.g., personal, writing, blogging, etc).

2. Set time for *everything*! My partner mocks me because I have activities such as "get ready for the day," "have breakfast," and "lunch at home" on my calendar, but that's how I know how long I should take to perform the next task and this way I have the satisfaction of having that empty spot on my calendar to decide what I want to do with it.

3. Schedule your whole week in advance. Trust me, even if you're still waiting on a customer's final decision about an important part of the project, or if it feels a little obsessive having your whole week planned out, if you already know what you're doing next, you become more efficient because you don't need to stop to make a decision every single time you finish a task, which frees your mind.

Having an organized schedule allows you to identify peak productivity moments and know which part of the day will be best for which activity. For instance, I usually prefer to have a packed agenda on Mondays, because I like to start the week strong by handling most of the heaviest tasks so I can keep up the workflow for the rest of the week.

Have a workspace that inspires you and keeps you focused

Whether it's a quiet home office, a busy coffee shop, or a library, find your perfect working space and invest some time in outfitting it. Maybe you want to paint the walls, buy a bookshelf, or invest in a portable laptop and carrying case.

At the beginning of my freelance career, I was in a mobile office style and would take my laptop everywhere. Soon I realized it was not easy to find a place with wi-fi in Luanda and I had to purchase a wi-fi mobile device, which cost me money each month. I soon realized this wasn't the best choice for my budget. Since I am more productive in quiet spaces, and making the space mine is very important for me, I need a clear space and quiet surroundings. I also noticed I love working with a view and in an open space, so four-wall working spaces are not for me.

You might be able to turn a veranda into an office or discover that shared working spaces are more your style, but don't forget you're at the beginning and you need to be very smart and strategic with your spending.

Don't forget about decorating and motivation. Personally, I'm still working on my current working space, but I know that it must have plants (both beautiful and proven to increase your creativity), a view, and a bulletin board where I can hang all my motivational quotes and images.

Choose things that make you happy and move you closer to your goal.

Keep in mind . . .

- Begin with the end in mind.
- Work at the same time as everyone else so you don't miss social time.
- Use a planner so that you can have guilt-free free-time.
- Build your freelance sanctuary.

CHAPTER 12

How to attract, manage, and keep customers

Goals set, check! New agenda, check! Workspace, check! Now it's time to learn how to handle your customers from the moment you identify your target market through your strategy for client retention.

Customer Attraction

Attraction is capturing the interest of your target client by showing the best of your attributes. This is the same technique you use in a romantic interaction, like a dance. Just apply the same principle with your customers, without the romantic part though! What I mean by that is you should aim for those who are already looking for you or who are connected to you through someone else.

This will require you to do two things: prepare and attack.

Preparation

Design your image

Think about how you'd like to be seen and perceived, how someone in your role should look in order to attract the target customer. Even though you are working for yourself, you are creating a business and you have to design the look of that business. What qualities do you want to project? Do you want to come across as fun and creative or elegant and professional?

Create a logo. It doesn't have to be complex and expensive, but I really advise you to create one because this will be proof to your prospects that you're a professional and take your career seriously. Even if it's your signature, your silhouette, a drawing you did when you were five years old, your logo is your business identity, so don't neglect it.

I made the mistake of not working on my business image for too long, and if you're doing the same, this might mean that you're still in limbo.

You can make your own logo in free design makers' websites, which can take you a few minutes. I used Canva because I like the fact that you can start from scratch and add every single element of your logo. But to find other services, just google "free logo design makers reviews" and evaluate the best service for you. While you're at it, don't forget the other elements of your image: contact information, address, social media, etc.

However, if you prefer to have someone design your logo and business stationery for you, there are sites like Fiverr.com where you'll find professionals available to work at lower rates. All you need to do is give them detailed information about your business, yourself, and your vision, and keep in constant communication. Deliveries are often made in as little as 24 hours.

With those elements created, you can then make your business cards, which are a good idea for physical interactions. They give people a tangible reminder of who you are. If you choose to leave the back of the card blank, you can write a personal note on it when you give it out. Make sure it's clear who you are and what exactly you do. You can print them yourself by using a Word template of your choice and you can also print a few at a time before going to a networking event. Make sure to always have a few with you because you never know when you will meet a potential client.

Create a free and consistent marketing strategy

Use the social media accounts you already have to attract clients by giving them a more professional look and making it clear what you're doing and which kind of work you're looking for. Also, don't forget to leave your contact information in a visible area so people can easily get in touch. Connect with all the people you know who may become clients or provide you with a lead. Surely most people know someone who needs your services.

The smart thing to do with your social media pages is to use strategic keywords for your description to attract the right viewers. Check the pages of other professionals in the sector and write down the three most used words and use them on your profile as well.

Remember to check if your picture looks professional, yet friendly. It should align with your business. If you're a travel writer, you can add a picture of your travels; if you're a photographer, show how you look in your element. The most important thing is that your face is visible and clear.

Next, I'd advise you to create a website. Having a clean professional website is key in establishing yourself as an expert in your field. It doesn't have to be elaborate and can even be a single page. People want to know who you are, what you do, and why they should hire you instead of someone else. Make the process clear for them so they know what it will be like to work with you. Find a few websites you love and write down what you like about them. There are a number of platforms that make it easy to design your own website even for free. Check out Squarespace, Wix, and WordPress.

You can also add a blog or social media page solely dedicated to your business. Creating useful content establishes you as an expert in your field and shows people the value you offer. Change your professional status and try to get as much visibility as possible. There are literally hundreds of websites and books about how to get attention on social media. Go for them! To minimize your time creating content, use programming apps that will automatically post your content for you. Try setting a post or twon a day for a month. Then, sit tight and focus on your core activity.

You can also send out personalized emails to your friends and family to let them know you're freelancing full time. Referrals can take you a long way and word of mouth is still the best marketing strategy (and it's free).

The most important thing, though, is that you figure out what channels your target audience would use to find you. It doesn't matter if you're everywhere if your target audience is not looking for you. Make yourself easy to find where your customers would search.

Have a customer attraction strategy

That will have a lot to do with pricing. It's important that you know how you'll want to position yourself in the long run.

In *Rich Dad's Before You Quit Your Job*, Robert Kiyosaki says that when you position yourself on the low-cost shelf, you'll be constantly battling with others for lower costs; if you position yourself in the middle, you become invisible and nobody knows who you are, whereas if you position yourself at a high cost, you have less competition but get fewer customers.

From my experience, the customers who were willing to pay the higher rates were the ones I never heard complain and even insinuated they could pay me more if I wanted.

When people value your work and have the financial affluence to afford it, they won't come to you looking for the best bargain but expecting the best service. This is obviously tied with experience, so know where you intend to get, to take small steps in that direction.

You can also apply some discounts and promotions such as buy one get one free or giving them a discount on a future purchase if they refer a customer to you.

I started by offering the first job for free (conditions applied) to give the opportunity for the customer to know my potential. It was as if I had to prove myself to them in order to gain their trust, and that was exactly it. But I was just starting out and had very little experience in the business, so I felt that was the best way to go about it. If you do have a lot of experience in your freelancing field, going cheaper may not be the smartest move, given that raising prices is another challenge.

Time to go for the kill

Use freelancing platforms

There are dozens of freelance work websites for virtually any job. You can use them to put yourself out there and get the attention of potential customers. I have used Upwork,

Translations café, Truelancer, and Freelancer, and have heard that Reddit is a great source of customers for freelancers as well.

All you have to do is set a detailed account, which looks very much like a CV, upload relevant work experience or your portfolio, and activate notifications for the jobs that interest you.

Freelance platforms disadvantages:

— The competition is fierce since there are hundreds of other freelancers submitting for the same job

— The rates are not the best, since you are often competing with inexperienced professionals who command a low rate, or you just get paid for a single task

— You might come across a scam listing

Advantages:

— This is probably where your chances are higher to land jobs, especially in the beginning

— You get to practice your pitching skills before aiming for higher targets

— You can practice negotiating

— It's low risk, especially when it comes to getting paid, since it's done through the site

— You have the opportunity to build a portfolio very quickly

To make this action more effective, choose one type of job at a time, for a period of time and set a minimum number of pitches you'll send per day. For instance, if you're offering freelance writing services, focus only on the blog posts for one month until you start pitching for magazine articles. Send ten pitches a day and go do something else, such as taking a free course in blog posting skills.

This will allow you to become faster at what you do and dedicate some time to your training. In the long run, you'll become an excellent freelance writer with expertise in more than one area. Speaking of areas of work, try to focus on a maximum of three. It makes you less believable if you're a specialist in ten writing areas.

Network, both to get customers and to know the competition

Networking is a fancy term for "meeting people with an objective in mind," but not in a bad way. It just means you'll be more intentional when saying "hi" to someone and shaking their hand. Watch your body language and look the way you know someone would if you feel compelled to do business with them. However, don't forget that your appearance will make your potential customers look at you, but your attitude is what will make them talk to you.

But even before going to external events, make the most of the contacts you already have and get closer to them. At the beginning stages, try to avoid distance communication and bring the most influential people in your network physically closer to you. Invite them for a coffee or even a beer, ask them questions and let them know what you're doing. Just don't ask for work.

If you're going to a very specific networking event with a defined topic and audience, do some research beforehand; it'll be a great conversation starter and will make you look knowledgeable. But don't talk all the way through the interaction. People like to be heard. Ask questions and show interest in people's lives and their work. Find out what it is they need and this way you can easily identify your precise targets.

There are so many ways for you to network! Put yourself out there. Use Instagram to find like-minded freelancers, Facebook groups, meetups, associations, you name it! The magic of social media works in a way that if you simply befriend someone with similar interests, it enriches your events and profiles suggestions. You can also become an active member of an association, group, or team to be able to organize meetings you'd like to attend where you'll invite experts to exchange knowledge. The sky is the limit!

The best of all those networking activities is that you will, most certainly, meet like-minded people who will either become your customers or recommend your services and, most times, your participation will be free of charge. Having fun will be the perfect icing on the cake!

Going straight to the source

Yes, it's as bold as it sounds. From the moment you feel confident enough to approach high targets, go for it, even if you're at the very beginning of your career.

Ashley Crouch, a visibility strategist, in her book *Unknown to Unforgettable,* says that for you to be noticed, you don't have to start small. What you need is to have a very clear goal and ambition. Sometimes you have to be brave enough to pitch directly to the intended target rather than work your way up through smaller jobs.

Tactics Ashley suggests:

1. Do some "healthy" stalking of your target

Suppose you, as a freelance writer, want to publish in *Forbes* Magazine. All you have to do is read their website consistently, subscribe to their magazine, and spot the most interesting articles to you. From the editorial information, you can see the names and often emails of the people in charge. Find them on LinkedIn and befriend them. See what they post and interact by commenting and liking.

2. Make them notice you

Very often high targets are people who get invited to speaking events, public interviews, or live events in general. Attend them, ask smart questions if there is a Q&A session and stay after the lecture or presentation to talk to them in person.

3. Give before you ask

As soon as you feel the moment has come, get in touch directly with them and show appreciation for their work even before talking about you. In short, make it about them. Then, offer a service for free, something that is actually valuable for them (e.g., an article on an exclusive subject) and don't ask for anything in return.

For some people in the high position, being contacted by a "nobody" can be considered annoying, but if you do it right and truly pay attention to their needs, you may be exactly who they wanted to talk to.

Keep in mind . . .

- Books <u>are</u> judged by their covers. Make a killer entrance!

- Marketing can be free, just learn how to get to your target audience.

- Make yourself visible even from the moon.

- Network = a closely connected group of people that exchanges information, expertise, and potential customer contacts. Go mingle!

- Aim for your target; don't waste precious bullets shooting in every direction.

- Don't let high targets intimidate you. They say the best perfumes come in small bottles.

Customer Management

Going back to that romantic dance I talked about in the attraction phase, now it's time for you to get to know your potential client and let them see you for who you are. This is when you let each other in and take a closer look.

Be communicative, transparent and define your conditions right from the start

The other day, I had the opportunity to watch a communication game called the *Two Bells*. If you haven't played it, I totally encourage you to, to understand the importance of communication on a deeper level. It was to test the communication skills of different groups.

It's a group game where an individual (A) assumes the role of a manager and an individual (B) is the employee. B has to leave the room and the manager has to designate a simple task for them to do when they return to the room, such as touching the table, touching a person in the room, or simply standing in a specific spot. The task has to be very simple and the rest of the group cannot interact with the employee when they return.

Here is the catch: the only means of communication between the manager and the employee is a bell. Exactly! No talking, no nodding, no signing, no expressive body language. The only thing that "talks" is the bell.

Once the mediator has explained all the rules of the game to the group, with participant B away from the room, it's time to go meet them alone and tell them that when they get back into the room, there will be a mission they will have to accomplish, but they will only know if they are going in the right direction when the bell rings. When they stop moving, the bell stays silent; if they move in the wrong direction, the bell stops. The bell only rings if they are going toward the mission. They can't talk, gesture, or ask for clues either. It's a version of the hot and cold childhood game, if you've played it.

Now you can imagine the amusing chaos this exercise results in. The employee moved around the room aimlessly, would go around and around the table looking expectant, but confused. Different managers would try different techniques like ringing the bell more viciously as the employee was getting closer. The remaining participants would either laugh or agonize with the employee. It was a roller coaster of emotions. In the end, the employee would get frustrated and give up, in almost every group that played.

How do you think they both felt? What did the other participants think? The answers to those questions are the same for you and your customer if you only use a bell to communicate.

Be specific, clear, ask as many questions as you find necessary to make sure you know exactly what you're doing. I know that often there is an assumption that you should know everything by heart and asking questions equals lacking knowledge and that's seen as negative. But you only keep evolving if you keep learning.

Besides, your customers will, most likely, be human beings, and those have all their own particularities and wants. You'll constantly be faced with different demands and singular requests. Just admit that this is new for you and be proactive: show that you are working to do it the best way possible.

You also need to set your conditions from the beginning for the customer to understand which kinds of requests you are willing to take, and which are completely off the table. Setting clear boundaries is part of good communication.

Learn to negotiate

Making customers understand that what they are asking for is humanly impossible is no easy task. Nonetheless, it is perfectly possible to walk them through your assessment process and make them see things from your perspective.

For instance, if a customer asks you to do a three-day job in just 24 hours, explain to them why you will charge more or why the minimum amount of time it will take is 48 hours.

In general, what tends to happen if you comply with such extraordinary demands is that the quality of your work can be compromised and that doesn't just affect that specific customer but could negatively affect the future of your entire career.

Try to be as clear and honest as possible and never imply in words or gestures that your customer is the crazy one. You can always analyze the work carefully and make suggestions (e.g., Can I deliver the job in chunks?). Making suggestions will show them you care and you're interested in completing the task. The conditions must be favorable for both.

Trust your instinct

The more you use your instinct, the better it gets, and it'll become easier to make decisions about clients, suppliers, partners, and every other aspect of your business that requires you to make a judgment call.

Once I received this email from a fellow freelancer offering me some work to share. She had a massive job opportunity from a big company. They wanted it to be delivered in record time and claimed it was a test which, if she passed, she'd become their exclusive provider in those services and I'd get more work through her. She was excited and certain I was going to accept.

But something didn't feel right and I had read somewhere that freelancers should avoid long testing projects because they were likely scams. I just couldn't see past it, even though the promised reward would be worth a whole year's earnings.

When I asked her which company wanted her to do this "test," I connected the dots. It was a big local company which I knew was not very ethical with its providers. It was clear to me why my red light went off on this "too good to be true" opportunity. She decided to proceed without me and two years later she told me the horrible experience she had with them.

On the other hand, your instinct might also tingle at good opportunities that may not look profitable at first. Just trust it!

Ask for feedback

Sometimes the fear of getting a bad response may lead us to overlook the real need to ask for feedback. Different cultures also shape how we regard feedback. In Angola it is not encouraged at all. Even in the professional arena, performance appraisal systems and practices are a luxury of the few companies that are trying to break boundaries and are having a hard time doing so.

Focus on the long run and think about how much better you can get if you learn exactly what your customers' needs and expectations are. You can be the next Bill Gates, just because you mastered the art of listening.

You have the freedom to choose where and how you want to ask for feedback. You can develop a small survey to send to your customers right after the conclusion of your project, or just ask a few questions in an informal way during your last interaction with the person and in private.

Get your survey template from my resources page: https://pessimainfeliz.com/resources/.

Just keep the message short and straight to the point, as you're probably writing to a very busy person.

It's just as crucial that you know how to react to the feedback you get. As a rule of thumb, when I receive only positive feedback I reciprocate, saying something nice about the person as well. For feedback on my improvement areas, I thank them and promise to improve, which I mean for real.

Unfortunately, not everyone sees the importance of giving feedback, so you may get just a few responses. To have more engagement, you can try offering a 5 percent discount on the next services or products you have to spare. Nevertheless, make the most of them and keep improving.

Keep in mind . . .

- Effective communication will take you a long way.
- Setting clear boundaries avoids misunderstandings and false expectations.
- Develop your instinct. Bad intentions hate a smart target.
- *Feed* = give food; *back* = in return. Ask for food for your business!

Customer Retention

And the dance continues . . .

At this point, you know each other and it's time to convince that person to spend the rest of their life with you. How would you convince them?

Keep in touch

In Portuguese, there's a saying, "Who come up come fed up," which means that it might not be a good idea to send three emails a day to your customers (unless you're working on a project that requires it). On the other hand, who doesn't come up will be forgotten, so make sure to stay present in your customers' lives.

To do this, you can wish them well on their birthdays or bank holidays, comment on their posts if you're friends on social media, or just WhatsApp them once in a while to share something you believe they would like. Texting simply to say "hi" is a valid option as well, if it's a long-term client and you feel your relationship allows you to do so. Use the *Reminder app* on your phone and set alarms to make sure your customers don't forget you and do keep building a solid foundation of trust and care.

Personally, I'm quite bad at this staying in touch part of the business, always finding the next bad excuse. I promise you I will get better at this today! Want to join me?

And, hey! While you're at it, stay in touch with your friends and family as well. It is nice and might even attract more business for you.

Dealing with customers equals dealing with emotions

Empathy comes from the Latin Greek *empatheia*, from em = "in" + pathos "feeling," which means the ability to connect with others' feelings. You're dealing with people on a professional level, but they have personal lives, goals, values and the same personality, regardless of personal or professional interactions. That said, it's natural that sometimes they feel emotional and anxious, or that they don't treat you the best way, without telling you exactly what you've done wrong.

To handle that, make sure to make an effort to know your customers a bit better to be able to predict their behaviour. Read between the lines, let them express themselves, do not judge them and never assume anything. Listen, decipher, interpret, act!

This long-term customer of mine is very kind and her way of showing appreciation for my work is by giving me gifts, anything she believes I'll like; she gives me something every time we work together. At first, I thought it was just a cultural thing, since we are from different countries, and in response, I'd make time in my agenda to do something fun with her.

She enjoyed it and was chatty and open to new experiences. However, nothing compared with the sparkle in her eyes when

I gave her a personalized key ring, with an African print dressed doll I had painted myself. She sent me pictures of it almost every day for a whole week, saying nice things about the key ring.

It was then that I remembered the book *Five Languages of Love*, by Gary Chapman, where he talks about the five main ways people feel loved: quality time, words of affirmation, gifts, physical touch, and acts of service. He explains that, similar to our mother tongue, we understand and perceive the message (love), if it is communicated in a language we can understand. That is, she would buy me gifts, expecting I'd do the same because that's how she feels loved and how she knows how to love best.

For me, making and spending time with a person, especially after I became a freelancer, is the most precious thing I can do for someone. It's not that we both didn't appreciate what we gave each other but understanding in-depth how to make the other person feel loved strengthens the relationship and turns it into a life-long commitment. This is how you get loyal customers.

Remember that humans are essentially emotional. Adopt positive words and pleasant language, always thank them for choosing you and stay professional but not robotic.

If a customer gets upset with you for a particular reason, acknowledge their negative emotions before trying to fix your mistake. That is a way to illustrate that empathy we talked about earlier and to set firm grounds of understanding.

I do know that being charming may feel natural for some, while for others it feels like the equivalent of climbing Mount Everest. To make this task easier, it always comes down to acting with intention and empathy. For that, there are a few techniques I apply, which are based on the book *How to Win Friends and Influence People* by Dale Carnegie:

1. **Try to always use the person's name or title** depending on the level of formality they prefer. But don't just say it, pronounce it the right way, especially if it is a hard name for you.

2. **Remember people's names** since it shows they are important to you. There are a few techniques for that, like looking into their eyes or associating it with something remarkable for you (e.g., Winnie, like Winnie the Pooh). One that works well for me is knowing the name of the person before meeting them in person. Find yours.

3. **Listen to them actively** and with a genuine interest in what they're saying. That is, don't be thinking of an answer while they're talking to you. Try to repeat what they are saying in your head or paraphrase out loud. That gives you time to process and makes the person you're speaking to see you're paying attention.

4. **Smile!** Yes, show those teeth even if you're on the phone. It's been proven that smiling affects your mood to the point that it can be heard over the phone.

Whichever techniques you use to improve your business relationships, be authentic and don't ever try to manipulate others because they will know.

Implement feedback, inform your customers and thank them

Another smart move to show your customers you want them to return is by implementing their feedback and letting them know of the result. Just thank them for their suggestion and tell the story of the new improvement. Even if it's something that won't be permanent, simply explain how you came to the realization it wouldn't work and share your findings. People like to feel they've been heard and also that you've got the autonomy to evaluate your "hows" and perfect them.

Keep in mind . . .

- Having a history with repeated pleasant moments will make people remember you fondly.

- Deal with emotions first, then with practicalities.

- Feedback then, more feedback.

CHAPTER 13

Develop a work methodology

Happy customers, happy business, right? Only as long as you keep your promises and meet their demands. Developing a work methodology will not only simplify your life by standardizing your tasks but will also allow you to leverage the 80/20 rule to make you more efficient.

The 80/20 rule, also known as the Pareto Principle, is about working smarter, not harder. It says that "80 percent of your results are generated from 20 percent of your efforts." That applies in every area of your life and can be translated simply into maximizing your impact in the most important and relevant areas, in order to achieve better results.

For instance, if you realize that you are naturally more productive during the two first hours of the day, do the most important or most difficult tasks in that time slot. Leave everything else for later.

Define how much you can get done in a period of time

With the good fortune of having practiced my work while I was an employee, I could comfortably estimate how many words I could translate a day or even how long it took me to write an article, and that allowed me to know my delivery capability and also made me sound professional to my customers.

When they feel you know what you're doing, they start trusting you and become more relaxed and flexible.

Monitor yourself for some time to understand what you can realistically promise your customers.

Get your productivity tracker template from my resources page: https://pessimainfeliz.com/resources/.

As a business, set weekly calendar times for working

Yes, now you have to take care of your product, your customers, your finance and your marketing. Don't panic, it's not as overwhelming as it sounds . . . if you schedule everything and do it regularly.

The actual work on your projects should take approximately 70 percent of your time. The remaining 30 percent, should be spent on building and strengthening customer relations, marketing, processes, and finances. However, in the beginning, this ratio can be more like 90/10, since you need a solid business to show for.

You can set this up however you like. Maybe you devote one hour each day to the 30 percent tasks or one day each week. Your agenda may look something like this:

1. Mondays

— Work: 8–12

— Lunch: 12–1

— Marketing: 1–2,

— More work: 2–5

Tuesdays

— Work: 8–12

— Lunch: 12–1

— Finances: 1–2

— More work: 2–5

2. Mondays

— Marketing: 8–10

— Customer relations: 10–12

— Lunch: 12–1,

— Processes: 1–3

— Finances: 3–5

Tuesdays–Fridays

— Work, work, work!

These are just suggestions; you may find your pace is different and even hire people who will deal with the non-core parts of the business.

The schedule doesn't need to be super strict, but if you stick to it, you'll see that you will reduce stress and anxiety a great deal by always having everything well organized.

Reduce distractions

It goes without saying that you need to stay focused, but it's easy to get distracted, so here are a few tips:

1. Turn off notifications

I know you'll say that a customer may call or text and it can be very urgent, but you can customize your notifications to be able to hear only the ones you consider a priority. Also, doing your work is just as important, but make sure you let everyone know how they can reach you in case of an emergency.

2. Use productivity techniques such as the Pomodoro Technique

Simply put, 25 minutes of focused work for 5 minutes of rest. Do this for two hours and take a 15–20-minute break. You can adjust this to your productivity rhythm. Just don't let any distractions get in the way of your focusing time.

For me 45 minutes of focused work then a 15-minute break works better because writing is a kind of job that needs mental warmup, and by the time I'm at my peak, it's been 10 minutes at least. Plus, I'm a sociable and active person, so after sitting for 45 minutes, it feels good to walk around and make a few calls while standing. My coworkers at the shared working space really like chatting with me, so this way I don't have cut them off after 5 minutes.

3. Set a time to read emails

This was a game-changer for me. All I did was book time slots in my calendar to read emails and set an automatic reply so my clients would know when to expect my replies and wouldn't be anxious not getting a response straight away. My email reads as follows:

Hello, how are you?

*Thank you for contacting me. I would like to inform you that **I only read my emails twice a day: at 9 a.m. and at 2 p.m. (GMT +1)**, in order to be more productive.*

Therefore, as soon as I read your message, rest assured I'll reply as quickly as I can.

I appreciate your understanding and wish you a nice day.

Best,

Winnie

Notice that I specify the time zone, since I have customers from different parts of the world. I also explain very briefly why I've decided to read my emails only twice a day, which helps the customer to be understanding. After all, I'm not reading my emails because I'm working on the task he/she asked me to do.

Reassuring them that I will reply to their email when I read it shows concern and care for their need to communicate, anticipating and dissipating anxiety.

I actually have my phone number as part of my signature, but I didn't say calling me was an option to give the receiver a chance to evaluate for themselves how urgent the matter is.

In 99 percent of the cases, your customers will respect your working time and wait until you answer their emails. You'll notice the world keeps turning without you . . . it's sort of liberating, really!

If you work from home, let everyone know you should not be disturbed or choose a time of the day you know you'll be alone. It will take some time before your family learns that working from home does not equal having to respond to every single calling, but be strong and remind them of the importance of your work as many times as you have to.

Learn how to analyze the service you are asked for

Since I have stopped taking translation jobs to dedicate all my time to blogging and to scribing this book you're enjoying so much, I usually refer other translators to my customers.

The other day, one of my main clients asked for a big translation job. I asked around and found another translator for the task.

On the date of the delivery, I realized she hadn't translated all the excel sheets sent and that almost compromised the client's presentation. The project was completed late, and the quality wasn't top-notch either.

In the end, she gave my client a discount and we knew it had been an honest mistake. Nonetheless, it was perfectly avoidable and the impression it left can never be erased from my and my client's memory.

To avoid situations like this, I strongly advise you to have scanning questions to evaluate what you're being asked to do and to make sure you and your customer are talking about the same thing and speaking the same language. Develop a sequential number of four or five questions that will allow you to assess the material so you can better estimate the delivery date and what the job will require of you.

In my case, I start with very open questions, depending on the details of the job. Asking about the exact needs and expectations of the customer might be a good starting point. You can then talk about deadlines, job details, and payment methods.

Here you can identify the main components of my short questionnaire:

1. **Customer needs and expectations:** What is the specific format, preference for a tool, budget?

2. **Deadline:** By when should the project be delivered? Should it be delivered in chunks or all at once? How negotiable is the deadline?

3. **Working conditions:** Is there a contract? Will I have to work on their premises or mine? Will food and transportation be provided? Can I have access to the materials beforehand? How about confidentiality?

4. **Payment methods:** Cash, card, bank transfer, currency; installments or one payment; upfront or after completion?

From those initial questions, you can then draw more questions, according to the nature of your job.

Be honest: don't agree to deadlines that you know you can't meet

It is scary, especially in the early stages of your career, but please say an honest "no," rather than a compromising "yes." Think long term and know that a satisfied customer equals 10 new customers, whereas an unhappy customer equals the loss of 10 potential customers. Therefore, don't be afraid to say no when you know you won't be able to deliver.

The best way I use to avoid a professional gaff is to estimate 20 percent more time than I think I will need. If you don't know how long it should take, google it! Seriously, it has saved my life so many times.

Write reports and build a portfolio

When I worked as an intern for a Parisian company, I remember getting annoyed by the need to constantly fill in those reports about everything my boss decided to measure. Six months after my arrival, a customer called asking for a quote for a project.

I went to my boss to talk about the customer and when I mentioned the name of the company, my boss asked me to check the customer relations file and there it was: that customer had had a terrible argument with my boss and still owed the company some money. That's when I understood why my boss kept such detailed reports about every activity on the business, from productivity to customer relations.

I'm not going to lie to you: reports are boring! But they give you a panoramic view of your work and prevent you from falling into old traps. Additionally, they will help you keep track of your work and see its progress, as well as identifying trends in your demand or market behaviour.

Make productivity reports, financial reports, professional relations reports. If this is too boring for you, pay someone else to do it. In fact, nowadays there are quite a few apps that can do it for you. All you need is the discipline to keep inserting the numbers to produce an analysis.

Similarly, keeping a portfolio will be a way to show your history to your potential customers. Spend some time building one; it can actually be very simple. If you don't have a website yet, simply have a PDF with the necessary information. You can even turn it into a web page, to give it that extra touch.

Other options to use as a portfolio are your LinkedIn page, which you can even add the links of your samples and Pinterest, which would be more useful for a more visual portfolio.

Your portfolio should include:

- A nice, clear picture of you
- A brief introduction of yourself, where you can include your vision and values
- Professional summary, stating what you've accomplished so far
- Certifications or main skills
- Professional goals
- Work samples
- Testimonials, if possible

If you go with the PDF version of your portfolio, keep it one page long and straight to the point. As you evolve, keep changing it and add as many links as possible.

Keep in mind . . .

- Measuring your response capacity will make you more productive.

- Remember, you should run your business the same way you'd like a five-star company to handle you.

- Patronize your processes so that you can expedite your work.

- A distraction-free environment will lower stress levels.

- Over-deliver and under promise.

- Boring reports will result in exciting business presentations/portfolio.

CHAPTER 14

Time management

You have methods in place, but the clock won't stop ticking. Time is on nobody's side, so you better learn to manage it wisely.

All of us have the same 24 hours in a day. If the richest people in the world managed to do all those amazing things in less than 1,500 minutes a day, why can't you perform simple tasks every day and make them grow into something great?

What you need to do is actually learn to prioritize well and act efficiently.

Start with the hardest things

Mark Twain said, "Eat a live frog first thing in the morning and nothing worse will happen to you the rest of the day." Then a few decades later, Brian Tracy went even deeper and wrote a whole book on the eating a frog and titled it . . . guess what?! *Eat that Frog.*

Start with your most challenging task. This is very much linked to your goals. The clearer they are, the more specific your tasks will be and the easier it will be to execute them.

That is based on the theory that by beginning with the hardest thing, then you generate the energy and sense of accomplishment that will boost your stamina to complete the rest of your tasks that day. Once you've done the hardest thing you've got on your list, you feel relieved, you have that *woohoo!* feeling. You feel like "If I've done that, I can do so much more!"

So, imagine that your to-do list includes doing the dishes, writing an 800-word article, and calling your mom. Which one do you think is the hardest thing? Which one do you think you should begin with? The answer should always be what's hardest for you; sometimes that will mean the task you like the least and other times the one that would cause you more trouble in the future.

Also, I don't necessarily agree with Twain when he implies that the frog is a bad thing, the worst that can happen to you. I have more of a "this is going to be a great day" attitude. Thus, I start with a morning routine that will give me strength for the rest of the day and that doesn't, resemble eating a frog. Not that I have ever tasted one anyway.

The life SAVERS

My morning routine is based on the life SAVERS, a concept created by Hal Elrod in *The Miracle Morning*. If you haven't read it, great, you will pay more attention to my explanation. But seriously, just read it!

I started following this routine because once I read somewhere that "you should start your day the way you want it to end." That is, if you want to end your day with that same feeling of joy and contentment, you have to start strong and keep a consistent pace. Hence, I practice this routine, especially when I know I'm going to have a busy day.

Quickly, I'm going to explain the life SAVERS concept and how I implement it in my life:

— **S** for Silence

Silence for me represents meditation, but it can be anything for you. Basically, it could be something as simple as focusing on your breathing, in a very quiet place and just quiet your thoughts. Lately, slow and focused breathing has been my favorite meditation, given that it slows the blood flow throughout my body and ultimately my brain.

You can also use the five, four, three, two, one grounding technique, which is to help you focus on five things you see, four things you feel, three things you hear, two things you smell, and one thing you taste. You can choose the way you want to enjoy silence and calm your mind.

I find this extremely important in hectic cities like Luanda because it trains you to hit pause and watch things unfold without letting them affect you in a negative way.

— **A** for Aspirations

Basically, aspirations mean to really know what you want, what your dreams are, and put it into the Universe. For some, this is called prayer. Regardless of what you name it, the trick here is to trigger your brain to fixate on a target.

I read my personal mission statement as well as my contract of self-commitment to write this book and keep on writing.

In *Breaking the Habit of Being Yourself,* Joe Dispenza teaches meditation and focusing on one personality trait you'd like to acquire. Let's say you want to be more confident. You breathe in and say "confidence," breathe out and say "fear," or whatever feeling is in the way of your confidence.

Notice that it is imperative that you verbalize your aspiration; you cannot keep it in.

— **V** for visualization

Visualizing is a step beyond aspiring. In the visualization, you say what you see that represents your aspiration. For instance, if you want to be a freelancer, you envision yourself already not having to go to a nine to five job to sit in the office all day. Instead, you see yourself working on your own projects, on your own time. If you're a freelance photographer, see yourself walking around town, taking the best shots of the old buildings.

A while back, visualization was defined as the act of seeing yourself as being already what you wanted to be. For example, "I am a rich person," "I'm a healthy eater." However, it has been argued that seeing or talking to yourself as your ideal version of yourself tricks the brain to reward you in the present, because perception *is* reality for your mind — apart from the fact that it makes you sound a tad delusional, in my opinion. Consequently, people tend to feel good already and get a bit lazy to achieve the aimed goal.

What I advise you to do is to truly illustrate the actions that will take you to your destination. For instance, becoming a freelancer may require working extra hours, designing a strategy to capture customers, or getting a certification. Visualize yourself taking those little steps that will get you where you want to go.

— **E** for Exercise

This is self-explanatory, but if you're not the working-out kind of person, don't worry. What we're talking about here is actually getting your body to move, to get some adrenaline, endorphins, and energy flowing.

It can be something as simple as taking a walk, jumping a rope 20 times, or even four rounds of 10 squats if you feel like it. Playing with your children or dog counts as well. Just get your body moving so that it connects with your mind in a healthy way.

This is my first life saver of the day. I use an app to start the day waking up my body with a session of 30 minutes of exercise.

— **R** for Reading

Reading is also self-explanatory . . . or not. You can just grab something you want to read, such as a book, a magazine, or those articles you've been saving on Facebook.

I modify that one a little bit because I'm an audiobook worm. Try your own reading style.

• **S** for Scribing

Ok, this is just a fancy word for writing. It can be traditional journaling or any other form of written expression you'd like to use. You can grab an old notebook, or get a specific type of journal. There are goal setting journals where you can focus solely on your goals and track your progress, and others that focus on the improvement of your relationships.

I still go for the classic "Dear diary" kind of format. At the end of each entry, I include three things I'm grateful for. That reminds me that there's also a gratitude journal.

Basically, what you want to do here is get the words out of your head and on the paper or Word document. It will give you an overview of your own life and personal development.

Even though it's a *morning routine*, the good news is that you don't need to do it in the morning. Although I would encourage you to, since this is my lovely frog, do it whenever works for you.

Set priorities

You may be driven by the degree of urgency each task carries. Or its deadline. Let's say for instance, that it's a task that you know is going to take a week. Obviously, you will prioritize this task over one that takes just an hour.

One methodology that might be helpful is the one suggested by Stephen Covey in *The 7 Habits of Highly Effective People*. In the third habit, put first things first, he allocates tasks into four quadrants.

— **Quadrant one: Important and Urgent**

He claims this is the quadrant of crisis management activities. That is, when you're under high pressure, when you're dealing with something very demanding, that feels like firefighting. Those are tasks that you will have to handle immediately.

— **Quadrant two: Not urgent, but important**

In this quadrant, you focus on strategies that will prevent you from going into the first quadrant. For example, working one hour per day for two weeks on a project that is due in three would fall into this quadrant.

Think of quadrant number two as the anticipated actions that will prevent you from getting into critical situation mode where you won't be able to think clearly about what you are doing. Instead of being reactive, you will be proactive.

— Quadrant three: Not important, but urgent

These are the tasks you feel are very urgent, but you're not sure about their importance. I was once assigned the task of researching my former company's competition. The manager said it had to be completed by noon the next day.

The next day I arrive at the office at 8 a.m. and the first thing he does is give me a completely different task. When I asked about the last task, suddenly it was no longer urgent or even important.

Those deceptive tasks that are born as the most urgent things and die as if they had never existed fall here. Distractions such as answering messages on social media and emails immediately are good examples of this type of task. Avoid them as much as you can.

— Quadrant four: Not important, not urgent

Here you will have something like playing games or online shopping. This quadrant's activities are very much escapes and sometimes time wasters. I'm not saying you don't deserve your guilty pleasure of watching telenovela or even playing Candy Crush once in a while but bear in mind that in the setting priority process, you should limit your time for this kind of activity.

Covey even says that good managers will spend most of their time on quadrant two, where they focus on the important things, preventing urgent ones or minimizing the urgent tasks as much as possible.

Delegate or share as needed

The best managers know they cannot do every single thing and they need to delegate. Even when you are a freelancer, you may need to delegate some tasks.

For instance, accounting. You don't need to do your own accounting, if you don't want to. It can be time-consuming and ineffective. Bear in mind that you need to focus on the essential tasks that you do well. For the tasks that don't fall into those categories, delegate whenever you can because delegating will buy you more time, which may translate in more money.

For the first two years as a freelancer, I didn't write reports, although I meant to ever since I had started my career. However, being the tedious task it was for me, I dreaded it. Luckily for me, my sister had just finished university and accepted the challenge, since she had so much time on her hands.

There was this time I also shared work with a fellow freelancer so we could both gain visibility and accomplish the required task.

I would advise you delegate legal matters to a lawyer. Paying them to interpret laws and keep your business protected will save you more money than you spend.

Set your limits

Setting limits is just as important as being productive. By that I mean you have to know when to stop!

Part of setting limits is limiting what you are doing at any given time. It's very important that you set aside times not only for being productive, but also for eating, answering calls, meetings, and most of all, resting. That's why I have adopted the Pomodoro technique. It keeps me fresh for much longer and helps me know when it's time to either switch activities or stop working altogether. During breaks, I take a walk around or just stretch out to combat the numbness of my muscles.

Resting may even increase your productivity and effectiveness. A power nap can work wonders for focus, efficiency, and creativity.

I have noticed when I take breaks during the peak of my productivity, I'm eager to come back after my break because I'm returning to a pleasant moment and that doubles my motivation to keep working.

Figure out what works best for you. You need to take good care of yourself in order to be at the top of our game. See it as an investment in your health, the best way to avoid going to the hospital and paying unnecessary health bills.

Keep in mind . . .

- Eat that frog first!
- Urgency is the enemy of greatness. Focus on what's important.
- Be humble and ask for help when you need it.
- Don't forget you're human. Take a break or a few.

CHAPTER 15

Learn to take care of your money

Time is money, right? Simply put, once you learn to manage your time, you're more than fit to put your money to work.

Have a financial plan

This is where it gets fun! Planning how you will allocate your money, even before it makes it into your bank account, will save you from making rash decisions and spending money unnecessarily.

How much do you want to earn over a period of time? Do you remember that goal setting scheme about your financial goals we talked about? Now it's time to actually grab them and break them down into an action plan.

Ricardo Kaniama, in *La Chèvre de ma Mère* (My Mom's Goat), gives an example of how he allocates a certain percentage of his profits (after taxes and bills have already been paid) from his businesses:

— 10 percent to tithe

— 5 percent to charity

- — 20 percent to reinvest in current projects

- — 50 percent to invest in new projects

- — 10 percent to family expenses

- — 5 percent unexpected events

Notice that 70 percent of his profit goes back into the business to make it grow. As an independent professional, that might translate into maintaining old equipment, purchasing new equipment, and training. Always include training in investment plans and remember that taxes and business bills should be part of the non-negotiable expenses.

However, as a freelancer, that money allocation may feel unrealistic. If it is unrealistic for you, I advise you just save 10 percent of any money that comes in. That is, have only three categories: income, expenses, and savings. As soon as the money comes in (income), set 10 percent aside (savings), and only then pay the expenses.

Since I've grown a little obsessive with categorizing and allocating my money wisely, I follow a similar money allocation scheme by having several bank accounts, to immediately transfer the right amount to the proper account. That helps me know straight away how much I have to spend on that category. However, it's very important to have your financial goals well defined and clear so you know what you're saving that money for.

On your action plan, draw the exact steps to take to get there. For instance, working as a content writer, I know how much I charge per word, page, or project. Thus, if I set a goal to earn *X* amount of money in six months, I just have to work backward and calculate how many pages I should write per month. Time allotment for the achievement of your goals is a must!

That also means that you have to tightly control your expenses, not just at the beginning, but always. So, consider moving into a cheaper place and making budget cuts, even if it means no alcohol, no cinema, or just not doing anything that costs over a certain amount of money.

Kaniama writes about when he decided to save money. He stopped using public transportation and even wore old clothes. He only owned two pairs of trousers. His friends and family thought he was going a bit nuts and some friends even stopped hanging out with him. Those were his short-term sacrifices for life-long gains and abundance.

Identifying the need for an item

I'm a minimalist so I believe that in every area of your life, you can gain more by having less. I have developed my own methodology of identifying the items I truly need in my life and that applies to my business as well.

When I want to buy something, I put it on a list. I just let it sit there for a while and many times months go by without my thinking of it. Then, I ask myself a few questions in order to really identify if I need it in my life/business:

1. Why do I need this item?

That is, how is it going to serve me, which area or gap in my life is this going to fulfill?

For example, when I worked as a translator, there were times I considered buying a printer to be able to print translated documents and invoices.

2. How have I been living without it so far?

Still using the printer example, whenever I needed to use one, I'd go to cyber cafés, So I compared what I was spending on that to the cost of buying a printer, the paper, and ink.

3. How often do I need to use it?

Honestly speaking, I only used a printer maybe once a month or even once every two months. So, very little. Even if I needed it every month, I calculated I didn't print more than five pages per month. That is approximately $2 USD, which would be a total of $24 USD per year. A new printer would be about $50 USD. My decision was obvious to me.

Try to really be realistic and find as many alternatives as you can so you can control your budget and foment the growth of your business.

Set your minimum price

This can be quite tricky, and of course, you will instinctively compare yourself to others in the market with similar standards to yours. Try not to think too hard on what others are charging because you may feel that your time is more valuable, even when you are at the beginning. Additionally, you don't know all the elements of the equation, such as their background, financial needs, niche, etc.

As a freelancer, Google has helped me see what's being done out there and what parameters are used to estimate price. Then, I took that information and tested how it could work on Angolan grounds. If the project requires a special skill set, I usually will charge about 20 percent more than my standard rate.

Another way to calculate this would be by comparing how much you earned at your conventional job. This method is particularly easy if you're coming from a place of experience, if you're freelancing on something you did before or have been for some time. Assuming you already know how much you can produce per hour or day, calculate how much you would like to earn per period of time.

Just remember that the way you position yourself with price will define your target audience. Therefore, it will ultimately come down to your boldness and professional behaviour.

It's also important to be flexible and talk to your customers about costs whenever you have the opportunity to. Negotiation is something very sensitive, and I do agree with the Covey, in *The 7 Habits of Highly Successful People*, when he says that when you cannot reach a win-win agreement, many times no deal is the next best option.

For instance, not too long ago I was invited to work as an interpreter for a very prestigious event. From the beginning, the person who was trying to hire me wouldn't disclose the terms and conditions of the agreement, claiming he hadn't been given that information yet.

He sent the agreement only 48 hours before the event. The working conditions themselves were fine, but the rate was way below what I was willing to accept, and I was careful enough to send him an email with my normal rates when he first contacted me.

Given my experience and my knowledge of the task, I tried to negotiate with him and we got to a point where we both found that no deal was the best deal. I can honestly say that there was no resentment left. We keep exchanging job tips to this day.

Create a well-monitored budget

Yes, you need a budget for your business as well, especially if you have a very limited freedom fund. On the matter of remuneration, for example, it wouldn't be very smart to take money out of the business for yourself while it's not mature enough. As Kaniama would say, "Don't kill your goat, feed it."

Have a reinvestment list

Justify your expenditures as if you were making a pitch for funding. Writing a reinvestment priority list is a smart plan, so it is aligned with your spending needs. To draft such a list, you only need to take two steps:

1. Revisit your business plan

Check your growth and financial plan to align your goals and define the necessary steps to take to achieve them.

2. Use a prioritization technique

I've already shared two prioritization tools in this book. The first one in the previous chapter, in *set your priorities,* and earlier in this chapter in *identifying the need for an item.* For those two to be even more effective for your reinvestment priority list, add the cost factor very clearly. That is, how much will the item cost you cand how can you reduce the cost without compromising quality.

Another business prioritization tool you can use is the ICE, which is an acronym for impact, cost, and effort, meaning:

Impact — what impact will this investment have on my business?

Cost — how much will it cost and what will be the return on investment time?

Effort — how much effort and time is required to implement this investment?

To use this tool and interpret the result of the analysis, there is a framework that I found hard to understand, so I created my own interpretation reading method.

The way I use it is to rate the impact, cost, and effort from one to ten, attributing the meaning that makes the most sense to me. For instance:

Impact = 1 (very low impact on my business); 10 (very high impact on my business)

Cost = 1(too expensive); 10 (I can definitely afford it)

Effort = 1 (massive effort and more than 20 hours to implement); 10 (effortless and less than four hours to implement)

Obviously, the ones scoring the highest would be on the top of my priority list. As a writer, a good example of an investment on my reinvestment priority list would be an online editing course. It would score nine on impact, ten on cost (I could probably get one for less than $10 USD), and eight on effort (it may take the whole four hours for me to digest everything and implement it).

You can get you ICE template from my resources page: https://pessimainfeliz.com/resources/.

Keeping such a list will give you extra time to think about what you actually need so if you come across a situation where you can get it for free or at a reduced price, you will know what to do. Just keep it easy to access, like on your phone, so that whenever you find yourself in a situation where you are tempted to buy something, you do so with purpose and an end in mind.

Allocate the right percentage by business area

Go back to your investment priority list and allocate them by area of the business. Let's say that you're a photographer. You cannot work without a decent camera, but considering you're starting as a freelancer and your budget is limited, do you really need white-balancing tools, camera straps, or any fancy materials, or can you work out a zero-cost alternative?

Make sure you prioritize the different categories, so you know what to invest in first.

For me, as a writer, books and training courses come first on my list, because learning and reading constantly makes me a better writer. Writing tools and programs come second because there are easy and cheap alternatives, such as Microsoft Word and

Google Docs. Having established this, I keep a list of books and training courses ready to cross one item at a time.

As you turn this budgeting and saving thing into a ritual, it will become automatic for you and you won't have to worry about where to spend your money.

Invest in your future!

Seriously! Investment has got to be the most underrated thing on the planet.

Let me just start by saying that to invest you don't need to:

1. Have a lot of money. (just any amount you can save will do)

2. Be a genius. (it's not what you know but what you do with what you know)

3. Be independent with no family to support. (just read *A Cabra da Minha Mãe*)

All you do need is the *investor mindset.*

Remember that you are now a self-employed person and that means you have to manage every single area of your life and spending your retirement money now will lead to deep disappointment in the future.

Therefore, investing is your best bet to conquer freedom. If you are at the beginning stage of your freelance career, master first the habit of saving money as soon as it makes its way into your account. Do not spend it! Repeat with me: "I will not spend investment money, not even for my wedding." For that, you should have another savings fund.

For starters, try to choose low maintenance investments. In many parts of the world, it is quite easy to have passive income from stock market investment, mutual funds, often controlled through apps or robot operated investment channels.

For you to check if investment opportunities are right for you and legit, please consider the following:

— As a freelance newbie, it will be smarter to invest only in passive income ideas. In simple terms, passive income is when you put your money in and collect the profits without doing anything or when very little maintenance is required. A few examples are:

   i.   **Rent your car** — Find a service you can trust, study the terms and conditions and make your car available whenever is convenient for you

   ii. **Convert your motorbike into a moto-taxi** — If you live in a big city, mobility might be a huge issue. Moto taxi has the added benefit of being a fast-moving vehicle, given the fact it doesn't get stuck in traffic. Find a competent driver and pay them on a commission basis.

   iii. **Lend money with an interest rate** — You can use websites such as Peer to peer lending, or just do it among friends and family, but make sure you draft a written arrangement for this.

iv.   **Sell an online course** — You may have to spend some time to set it up in the beginning, but all you need is knowledge on the subject and a word document.

v.   **Rent storage space** — Have a spare room but don't want to rent to a person? Rent it for people to store their belongings.

vi.   **Sell digital files on Etsy** — Is painting or photography a hobby? Maybe it can be profitable as well.

vii.   **Sell templates** – Remember all the business templates I mentioned throughout the book? Don't worry, I'm giving them for free, but you can make your own version and sell them.

But what if you want to spend zero time to create a passive income source and want to give your money to a safe entity to manage its growth?

For that, you have the so-called online investment websites or brokers, such as Betterment, Acorns, Coinbase, E.Trade, Ally Invest, among others. Do your research and find which one suits you the best.

Speaking of spotting investment opportunities, here are a few ways to identify if an investment opportunity is a bad idea:

- — **Unsolicited approaches** by any means of communication available, especially by an unknown institution.

- — **No two-way contact** when the institution doesn't allow you to call back or reach them somehow.

- — **Under pressure decision-making request** when you're forced to make a quick decision under the pretext that it's urgent and you'll miss out on the opportunity to make money.

- — **High return rate promises** that are much higher than the norm.

The best way to run from those scams is to do your research by using online resources (look for reviews on that investment opportunity)and talking to people about it, particularly to those who've done the same thing and ask for feedback.

But remember, the best investment are relationships. Your peers, the people you know, acquaintances. Those are the people who will definitely help you grow. If you know how to nourish and keep healthy relationships, the return will almost certainly be incalculable.

Investing should be one of your main goals because it's "starting with the end in mind," paying your business first and putting your long-term vision into practice by taking action. If it weren't for investing, I must say that funding my big goals would be next to impossible.

Keep in mind . . .

- Put your money on a timeline and you'll see it climbing up steadily.

- Know what your time is worth . . . monetarily.

- Hold yourself accountable for your budget.

- Investing is the key to set you free.

CHAPTER 16

What if I can't be financially independent after my freedom fund dries out?

I know how to be a freelancer, but I cannot be financially independent; my freedom fund is drying up. I'm just running out of hope. I'm running out of money and a bit of dignity as well. What to do now?"

Every one of us goes through ups and downs and they might feel more severe when you're a freelancer, at least in the beginning. Here is what I do when that happens.

When I found myself in that situation, the fight or flight instinct kicked in. What always helped was to look at my people, the brave Angolans who live below the poverty line and still have the strength to smile and the openness to share. Our *zungueiras*[2] bare more than any human being should, and they never give up. They are honest people who make a living from what they

---

[2] Women who are street sellers and carry their goods in a bucket on their heads all day long, walking around the city.

can, not having the opportunity to even be aware of their rights as citizens.

I think, if they can do it, what am I complaining about? and I also remember the responsibility of helping build a better country for them and their children. I have to act for those who barely have the opportunity to breathe.

Remember, if you're an Angolan citizen reading this book, you're probably one of the few who have the luxury of being able to read and get hold of a book, without having to think about how you'll manage to eat tomorrow. Look around, do you really think this is the worst situation you could be in?

Go for a walk

Something that you will find out from being a freelancer is that everything will be fine, regardless of how many times you feel like it won't, and I'm not trying to sugar coat this for you. Realistically speaking, you will discover there is always a solution.

There's a Portuguese saying, "What doesn't have a solution is solved." That is, the solution is already inside of you, just give it some time for it to come up. That's why whenever I feel down, I go for a walk.

Similar to the positive effects of exercising during your morning routine, moving your body when you're stressed out will ease your mind and help you think clearly. Like a magic trick, your mind will find creative and ingenious ways to address the source of your stress.

For you, it may be just getting out of the house and talking to your neighbours, or even joining your children in their fun game will help. The important thing here is to take your mind off your troubles and into a breezy place.

I would, however, advise against wasting your time on social media. That may even put more pressure on you when you see other people's "perfect" lives. Try to really be present and trust in your capability of building a better future for yourself.

Wake up early to think and clear your thoughts

Another way of tackling those problems is by waking up early. I really like sleeping; I love my bed. But remember that most of your life happens while you're awake. What you do while you are awake matters a great deal and will have a huge impact on your future, decisions, and financial growth.

Waking up early gives you the advantage of the morning quiet to allow your thoughts to flow.

During a rough patch in my life, I decided to try something new. I decided to wake up at dawn and go to the beach to exercise and think. Tough, but necessary. At that time of the morning, few people were out and the city was quiet and airy. The quiet allowed my heart to listen and my mind to speak. A solution to my troubles became clear. Digging my feet in that soft sand and looking at the vast sea made me feel part of nature, and that gave me peace. This practice has changed my life over the past years, and it aligns with my urge to feel part of something bigger than myself, which I consider therapeutic.

Invest in what you already have

Working longer hours, or getting a second or third job may be the go-to response when you are in a financially challenging situation. It makes you think that maybe you need to work more to earn more money. That can be one way to go, but it can result in exhaustion and frustration. Life is time and money doesn't buy everything.

Sometimes, the key is as simple as putting more thought into what you're already doing. That is, working smarter. Shifting to something new can sometimes cause more harm than good. That is why you need a plan and a support team before you decide to take the jump.

There are a number of studies that defend that focus is more efficient than time invested. So if instead of working 14 hours, you work eight hours with clarity and focus, you're much more likely to be efficient, which will result in growth and ultimately, financial flow.

Working as a freelancer, you will have a lot on your hands, and it's very easy to get desperate. If you don't get the exact results you have envisioned (and that's going to happen), you will feel pushed into a corner.

However, if you keep exercising the "it will be okay" mentality, you will find out that sometimes, all you need is to stop for a while. Give yourself the space to be really present with your situation or borrow another pair of eyes to really look into it and give another point of view.

Recently, I couldn't see how to stop providing translation and interpreting services but wanted so desperately to invest more time in writing and finally write my first book. During our monthly budget meeting, I expressed my desire and presented my options to my life partner. He simply said, "Why don't you simply write for a living?"

You see, I've been working as a content writer for three years, but because it was always something fun and sort of a side hustle for me, I never called myself a writer. Ironic how sometimes you're already living your dream without realizing it.

This is why it's important to have clarity on what you want so you recognize when it is becoming a reality in your life.

Is side hustle an option?

I know that the last thing you'll be thinking of is to do more work on the top of making it as a freelancer, but bare with me.

When I speak of a side hustle, I'm talking about you earning money with your hobbies. Yes, you read correctly! As a writer, I go through several books a month and spend some money on them.

However, a while ago I came across this website that pays you to review books. Simple as that. All I had to do was read a couple of books and follow the review guidelines to become a paid reviewer. I was already reading books anyway, now I just get paid for that.

With the need for visibility, many products and services need trustworthy reviews and many of them. Therefore, you have an opportunity to review items you're already using. And the best part, you'll make a few couple of hundreds per month.

Have a look at the fun jobs section of my resources page, to find a paid hobby fr you: https://pessimainfeliz.com/resources/.

You can always go back to the corporate world

Maybe none of the suggestions above have worked well enough for you, or you have just reached your breaking point and thought, "Maybe freelancing is not for me". Or maybe it is for you but because you didn't take the necessary steps before jumping into it, you need to go back to the corporate world, and then build up this freelancing career with a more solid foundation. Sometimes you need to take one step back in order to take two forward. You still will be employable, and sometimes even more than when you quit your job, because you will gain entrepreneurial skills, and those are rare and valuable.

If you know by now that you do want to be a freelancer but still don't have the foundation for it, view your conventional job as the fast track for you to be able to do well as a freelancer. So do not feel bad if you made the mistake of jumping too early. Consider it a learning opportunity. Every experience is valuable.

If after one or two years working as a freelancer it hasn't worked out, and you had to go back into the office, that does not mean you failed. It means you've learned for two years about what it takes to be a freelancer, and the best decision at that point was to go back to being an employee so then you could do better as a freelancer. The sky is the limit!

Keep in mind . . .

- Life is not a straight line, for any of us
- Moving your body can still your mind
- Search for answers in silence
- Value what you already have
- Monetize your leasure activities
- Going back is OK, at least now you know who you are and where you want to be

CHAPTER 17

Be scared but do it anyway!

You've become a freelancer, all is going well, you have your recurring customers, and now it's time to change!

For some of you, it may simply mean that you're going to become a company owner because your business grew exponentially and you want to grow with it or it may mean just a slight change in your services or products. Now it's time to identify the elements that brought you here and the ones that will push you further.

Focus on what you can do well and enjoy

Many times, because you're too scared of taking the leap or taking that step toward your dream, you just choose to do something that gives you a living and is more consistent, at least on the surface. But maybe all you need is a taking the first step.

For instance, the Brazilian YouTuber Whindersson Nunes has a very humble background and is now travelling the world just because one day he decided to sit in front of his camera and share with the world what he does best, which is making people laugh by making fun of his own reality. He took that seriously and the world took him seriously in return.

Today, he is the most popular Portuguese speaking YouTuber in the world. All he does is bring a little bit of Brazilian humor to Brazilians and other admirers around the globe.

Invest time, effort, and energy in what you truly love, and money will follow.

Make a gradual change and announce it

Once you know exactly where you want to go, you will need to be ready to leave some things behind. You may have to kiss employee benefits goodbye or you may have to drop a hard-earned title if you're entering a whole new field.

It doesn't happen overnight. Nature is clever in a way that makes all of us go through a process, the metamorphosis, before being ready to be the next thing. You're called an infant until you manage to speak and walk, then you're called a child and act silly and playful. When you start acting out and are a bit stupid and reckless while you battle your way through emotional roller coasters, you've earned the teenager label. The process is natural and needs to be embraced.

When I decided to transition into writing and took "author" as my new title, I first changed my email signature. That was just one of the scariest moments of my life, even though I knew hardly anyone would notice it. It was the first step in revealing my new identity to the world. I knew I'd better start preparing to answer questions: "Do you have a book?" "Can I read it?" "Where do I find it?"

Finally, as soon as I felt confident enough to clearly announce my change of career, I wrote a cheerful and grateful email to all my former clients, letting them know the details and offering help in finding my replacement. It's important to not leave them with a void.

Keep in mind . . .

- Control your path, but let natural elements play along
- Let everyone know who you've become. Who doesn't love butterflies?

PART III

After the Dark, There Is Light . . . Right?

"Tough times never last, but tough people do."

—Robert H. Schuller

CHAPTER 18

How the life of a freelancer actually is

"Now that I am a freelancer, I'm just going to live happily ever after." Well, first of all, happily ever after is something Disney made up . . . it doesn't exist. But, that's actually the beauty of things. You keep learning and then you realize you can keep growing and become a better version of yourself.

To be honest, freelancing life is not for everyone. I mean, the constant going after customers, not knowing how much you'll earn the following month, and having to make all the decisions about your career can be daunting. However, if you manage your time and money wisely, struggles will become opportunities rather than burdens.

Nonetheless, the bittersweet reality of freelancing is an emotional roller coaster. There will be times where you'll have moments of high and feel absolutely amazing, grateful, and invincible; there will be others where you'll feel the street dog is better off in life than you.

Whenever you feel down, just think of your why, your purpose. Think of it as a person, the personification of your foundation in life. Imagine you telling them how you feel, what you think, and your reasons for being such a wreck . . . tell them you're questioning your decision, doubting your capabilities, and thinking of quitting. Feel their eyes on you, their disappointment piercing through you and their tears dropping heavily on your knees. How bearable is it for you? How would you feel if your purpose thought they aren't valuable or important enough for you?

Doing this exercise of internal conversation gives me great strength and makes the challenges look small in the face of my defined purpose in life. It makes me think "I can do this. I just needed to cry a little to relieve the overwhelming emotions." In the end, I realize that choosing an unconventional professional career style makes me stronger every day.

For you to have a more realistic idea of what it means to be a freelancer, I have made a list of pros and cons, based on my experience and those of some of my fellow freelancers.

CHAPTER 19

Cons

Negativity showers

Family and friends will admire you for your courage but project their own fears on you, as well as their doubts and insecurities.

Being a freelancer represents a kind of freedom that many people might want to have, or dream of, but it is one thing to want something and another to go get it. And some people will reject those who are go-getters. You might be perceived as too aggressive, an anxious kind of person who cannot wait for things to unfold and want to make them happen instead. It might take some time for people to take you seriously, to believe in you as a self-sufficient professional.

Regardless of where you're from, the reality is that most people are comfortable with the way things are and aren't willing to change. Don't get me wrong, this isn't necessarily a bad thing.

But know that, when someone is negative about your freelance plan, it is out of their own fear that you will not succeed, the fear of the unknown. In the end, it comes down to you, evaluating what you want and what's best for you. You have to muster the strength to move forward, regardless of others' opinions, whether they're your parents, spouse, or friends; it comes down to your own definition of greatness.

Difficulty in attracting and keeping customers

Another challenge in the freelance world is the difficulty of attracting and keeping customers, especially at the beginning of your career, not to mention that dealing with them directly is a challenge in itself.

When you're unknown in your new field, standing out may be a tough mission. In such situations, aiming high on marketing is definitely a good idea and you don't need to spend much money on that.

You can use your freshness as fuel and make the most of your authenticity to attract people who appreciate your traits. Remember that people are people everywhere on the planet and they are all very particular. For instance, there are thousands of travel bloggers now, but how many of them are black, African, and actually live in their home country?

Pro tip: Find your niche and refine it to your advantage. Not only there are needs that have not been addressed, but there are those that have not been addressed well.

Discipline

The battle with discipline, time management, financial organization, and priority setting is constant. Discipline is often freelancers' hardest challenge. I'm talking about following a weekly schedule, waking up early, and sticking to a routine. I had to look into myself when I decided to become a freelancer and redefine who I was and what I wanted to become.

If you don't have a background that demanded discipline and consistency, they can be hard habits to acquire. If you're starting an independent career, I'd advise you take small steps to improve your organization and discipline. Create a weekly schedule for yourself and stick to it. After a month, you can assess how well it is working for you and adjust it as needed. Small steps like this will become a habit, and eventually a part of who you are.

If you're ill, your business stops

Unfortunately, this is the though truth about being a freelancer — no health, no wealth.

The best way to deal with this is to prevent yourself from falling sick. That is, keep a healthy lifestyle, wash your hands, eat well, rest, drink water and do follow your grandmother's advice when she tells you to eat all the veggies.

Nevertheless, I know better that sometimes this is not enough. If you do get sick, here's what you can do:

— Try reducing your physical activity, work from home, if possible, and drink tons of water.

— If you can't do any work whatsoever, let your client know.

— You can pass the project onto a fellow colleague and manage them.

If your client and colleague have to interact directly, choose a less experienced one, to reduce the likelihood of you being replaced.

Irregular earnings

As tough as it is, irregular earnings are very much a reality of freelance life. It's hard to know for sure how much you will make in a month. You no longer have that monthly salary and that can be uncomfortable and stressful at times.

To handle this, you want to go back to your financial plan, the one you wrote at the beginning of this book, and use it as your compass to guide you through your next financial steps. You should revisit it regularly, especially in the beginning, when you're still learning how to manage your money in the most effective manner.

Pay it a weekly visit, to check your progress and identify where you could do better. Make sure your plan is directly and actively contributing to your goal. Ideally, you should save up enough to cover your expenses for a few months, and it's important that you calculate how much that would be.

As you see, not having a regular income makes financial planning and a high financial literacy level all the more important. Ultimately, it will lead to better investments in yourself and your future and the realization that you will always have some money coming in. Think of it as a tree, and all you have to do is water it every day and take good care of it.

Goodbye office family

You will have to say goodbye to work-family as well. Giving up that part of your social life can be hard. We often don't realize the importance of the casual interactions we have at work.

Being a freelancer showed me the lonely side of professional life. It made me miss corporate life a little. But being very firm in my decision to making freelance life work, I knew going back wasn't an option.

To combat the isolation of freelance life, you can take up a new hobby or turn a current hobby into a group activity that will build up another family. For instance, if you like jogging, just get into a jogging group, where you can see each other a few times a week.

Another way out of the solitude of freelancing is the use of shared working spaces. They are becoming more popular and can serve as your new office. Equally, they can be a great way to network. If you can afford it, a shared workspace can be a great option.

Keep in mind . . .

- Being an outlier is not for everyone

- Be your boldest self and you'll get the best customers for you.

- Mini habits are solid roots for new great routines.

- Always put your clients first, even if it means losing them.

- Investment in your knowledge is the best way to prevent a financial downfall.

- Everybody needs a family, go build your new one.

CHAPTER 20

Pros

Time flexibility

Focusing on the good parts, time flexibility is just priceless. As a freelancer, you no longer need to ask for 22 days of holidays, you don't need to ask for permission to take time off work.

Frankly speaking, you'll probably have zero days of holidays in your first years as a freelancer, especially if you haven't planned it out beforehand. However, sooner or later, your body and mind will demand some rest from work activities and you'll remember that you can take holidays whenever you want.

Additionally, time flexibility is also about the power of using your time to serve your best interests. I once watched a video of a freelance social media manager who chose to work hard for one week a month and travel for the rest of it. So, she would put 30–40 hours of work in one week and explore different locations for the next three weeks straight. The important thing is to manage time wisely to maximize your productivity and the freedom of choice you have in your life.

156

Power of choice

And speaking of choice, guess what?! You can choose your customers, projects, working place, time of the day, dress code. The choices are endless.

Long gone are the days where you had to laugh at your boss's not funny jokes and deal with the same difficult customers every single day. As a freelancer, you can have the power to "fire" anyone who doesn't align with your business goals, including customers.

To illustrate this concept of "firing customers," Robert Kiyosaki in his book *Rich Dad's Before You Quit Your Job* told the story of how rich dad had to fire a difficult customer.

The customer was a guest at one of rich dad's hotels and at check-in, he refused to pay for his stay, demanding he had to test all the services to see if it was worth it. At check out, he paid only 50 percent of what was due, claiming the hotel was low quality. After weeks of tense calls between the hotel and the guest, they negotiated an amount for the guest to close his payment. Six months went by until this case was closed. The customer was blacklisted, aka fired from the hotel as a customer. No longer would the staff accept him as a client.

Precious time and energy were wasted on this situation when it could have been invested in delighting good customers, improving processes, training employees — in short, upgrading the whole company.

You have the freedom to both choose the customers you want to work with and also to decide if you want to invest time struggling with delayed payments. I know it can be hard to resist the urge of accepting a client who will supposedly pay you for your time, but don't forget the "trust your instinct" lesson. Don't fall for false promises. Exert your power of choice.

Unlimited earnings

For as long as you can be productive, you can earn money. Therefore, depending on how committed you are and on how much your customers are willing to pay for your commitment, you can earn as much as you can imagine. You're not bound to a salary, to a fixed amount per month anymore. You can now earn as much as you are willing to give.

If you invest in efficiency and expand your creativity, you'll be able to develop an endless money stream and literally have unlimited earnings. Make an effort to optimize your processes, your systems, and even your equipment so you can deliver a high-end product with little sweat.

Mobility & exploring

Having the freedom to work from literally any place in the world is very likely a top priority of most freelance professionals. Imagine you're a parent and have always dreamed of working from home so you can spend more time with your children. That's something that as a freelancer becomes a reality. You can now stay home and make the most of the first years of your little ones' lives. Or you've always wanted to travel full time and the office life makes you depressed. *Voilà*, freelancing is here for you. Nowadays, travelling *is* a job, so you have no excuse.

That's how I lived my first years as a freelancer and will still live many more to come. Especially if you work in a particularly creative sector, travelling enhances your creativity and ultimately makes you a better professional. More resourceful and daring. The human body was not designed to stay put for so many hours as the corporate world has dictated, so making the most of mobility can only bring you the best of what freelance life can offer.

While you're at it, explore your own curiosities. You know that secluded island or beach you've been waiting for the perfect moment to visit? Now is the time. You can visit that museum and work in their café for a few hours, you can rent a desk at a shared working space just to have a sneak peek at that cool place and how it feels to work there, you can go to that abandoned site by the mountain when nobody else is there and do some exploring during breaks. You get the idea.

More control over your present and future as well

Living a life of purpose and intention is most likely one of the main reasons you want to be a freelancer. Choosing to follow a different professional path from most people will lead you to evaluate your choices in general, in all areas of your life, such as housing, consumption, entertainment, etc. That is, you are more likely to start questioning all the patterns in your life because you've changed such an important one.

Consequently, your decisions will be guided by awareness and constant questioning, in search for the next version of what you want. For me, this is the definition of living with intention and having the willpower to make your dreams a reality.

Higher mental malleability

Mental malleability is what the science community calls *neuroplasticity* which, defined by the Oxford Dictionary, is "The ability of the brain to form and reorganize synaptic connections, especially in response to learning or experience or following injury."

Freelancing makes you face new challenges all the time. This challenges your mind all the time, pushes you to the edge constantly and forces you to go through at least one metamorphosis a week. Basically, you're a whole new person every month.

That's what freelance life gives you: it gives you the flexibility of understanding that even though you've gained more control over more areas of your life, you still need to come to terms with the parts that you cannot control, and also to learn to make the most of them. This is definitely the upside of freelance life that I appreciate the most. I really like the fact that whenever things go south, I still believe strongly there is a solution, I still see an opportunity for improvement.

No company to control

Ok. You're an entrepreneur, a *solopreneur*, to be precise, so you need to take control over your business and manage it in an efficient way. Even though you're doing most things alone, it does not mean that you're on your own and you know that. You can always outsource, create partnerships, or exchange in order to obtain what you need and contribute to the growth of your career.

I want to give back to the community with my work, and I've realized that there are a number of ways to do so. Freelancing has given me the opportunity to do that in the ways that work best for me.

Keep in mind . . .

- Time is at your mercy, but it won't stop for you.
- The time best invested is the time never wasted. Make wise choices.
- The more efficient you are the more you can earn.
- Expand your mind by exploring your surroundings.
- Living in the present will lead to a more promising future.
- Allow yourself to change so you can advance.
- Give your freelancing business the shape your hands can form.

Conclusion

Well done, you made it to the end! Thank you for sticking with me and for strongly considering my guidance in this career change. This is an important moment in your life, and I am glad you're investing the time to make well-informed decisions.

Getting to know yourself better will not only make the ground more solid for your next steps but will also give you peace of mind and a comforting sense of security that's hard to experience otherwise. During this journey, obstacles will become opportunities before your eyes, and you'll feel capable to grab them by the horn. That's why committing to your goals on paper is crucial in this process.

Likewise, facing your current financial situation will help you measure the risks and be prepared to mitigate them with the help of your findings in the research and in the exchanges with the professionals you'll come across. Remember that you don't have to do this alone; let your loved ones be part of this journey. After all, it will probably affect their lives as well.

If you dedicate enough time and energy to your business plan, rest assured that it will broaden your perspective, giving you a business mindset and putting you in the position of a business owner — one who now knows what to do to perform competently in each main area. Feeling like a pro already?

Time to test it all out and discover what works in your reality and what needs to be adjusted to give you a competitive advantage. For those who decide to invest 100 percent of themselves into freelancing, maintaining clear focus and actionable goals will help you avoid frustration and dramatically reduce stressful moments.

Don't be afraid of the "dealing with customers" part of the business, for they are what will keep your practice fruitful. Don't approach them as a desperate newbie. Treat your job like a business and they will see you like a businessperson. Additionally, don't forget to treat them like human beings because that's their essence and emotions are part of them. Address their feelings first in order to build authentic and strong relationships, which will sustain your business.

In the process of making yourself a better professional, implement practices that will simplify tasks and expedite repetitive activities to improve your results. Treat yourself as you would like a company to treat you as an employee and have systems in place to maximize your productivity, reducing room for procrastination. Also, catalogue your interactions and projects, building something impressive.

As a free professional, time is at the essence, which means managing it wisely is the only option. Therefore, setting your priorities straight and using the necessary resources to eliminate wasting time will help you get things done in a timely manner which, in result, translates into the freedom to do what you want.

Since your success will be in part measured by your finances, you must have a financial plan. Only if you have full control of your present you can start planning your future; this is where investing comes to play. Thus, invest to multiply your wealth, but always remember that investing in yourself is what will give you the essential equipment to reinvent your own person and leave your mark.

Make the most of freelance life to be with your loved ones and exercise your passion, and don't give up for as long as you believe it is possible. Put the pros and cons in the scale of life and know this: at the end of the day, it all comes down to your mindset, the lens through which you choose to see the world around you.

As soon as you feel ready, turn the page and say goodbye to your day job.

Your Next Steps

To grasp the contents of this book you only need to take six steps now:

1. Make a list of the exercises suggested in this book you'd like to do. If you're using the Dare Action Plan Workbook, they follow the order of the chapters, but you're free to choose which ones to do and in what order.

2. Access the resources page on https://pessimainfeliz.com/resources/to grab the list of resources I mentioned throughout the book and download the templates.

3. Set a deadline to digest and work through every part of the book, with the help of the resources. (e.g., Do the exercises and read the resources in reference to chapters one to five in one week, finishing by *date.)*

4. Set a deadline for the start of the trial period of your freelance business.

5. Find your tribe. Sign up to freelance groups and talk to them about your plans.

6. Set a deadline to get your business plan off the paper. Time to get started for real!

Acknowledgments

I would like to express my very great appreciation to Beacon Point LLC for their valuable and constructive suggestions during the writing and development process of this book. Their help in the editing part of this book was crucial for the completion of a quality writing piece.

ABOUT THE AUTHOR

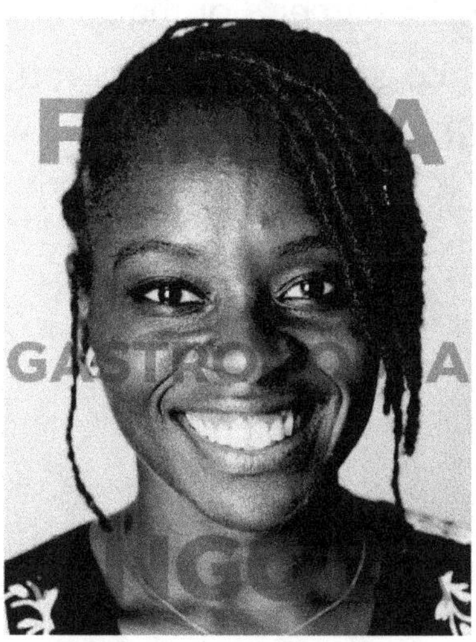

Winnie Carmo has been an independent professional almost as soon as she graduated. Being a free professional is all she knows as far as career ambitions go.

She started as a freelance translator and interpreter and worked for institutions such as Ministries and the UK Embassy. She then invested more time in freelance writing, publishing more than one hundred articles in English and Portuguese.

Her degree in Business Management and French studies was a solid foundation for her to successfully manage her own career and use the mastery of languages wisely. Her writing skills may be confirmed independently in her clients' platforms and her blog (www.pessimainfeliz.com).

A traveler and a foodie, Winnie has a passion for anything that resonates with freedom. As a 'Terrible Unhappy' as she calls herself, she's now committed to assisting Angolan solopreneurs who want a successful career. For that, she started a blog about her own journey into solopreneurship and how to unveil the mysteries of her birth country – Angola.

Can You Help?

Thank You for Reading My Book!

I really appreciate all of your feedback, and I love hearing what you have to say.

I need your input to make the next version of this book and my future books better.

Please leave me an honest review on Amazon letting me know what you thought of the book.

While you're at it, subscribe to my blog www.pessimainfeliz.com for more tips on how to make it as a freelancer.

Thanks so much!

Winnie Carmo

NOW IT'S YOUR TURN

Discover the EXACT 3-step blueprint you need to become a bestselling author in as little as 3 months.

Self-Publishing School helped me, and now I want them to help you with this FREE resource to begin outlining your book!

Even if you're busy, bad at writing, or don't know where to start, you CAN write a bestseller and build your best life.

With tools and experience across a variety of niches and professions,

Self-Publishing School is the <u>only</u> resource you need to take your book to the finish line!

DON'T WAIT

Say "YES" to becoming a bestseller:

https://self-publishingschool.com/friend/

Follow the steps on the page to get a FREE resource to get started on your book and unlock a discount to get started with Self-Publishing School